SOCIAL DEVIANCE AND THE HUMAN SERVICES

SOCIAL DEVIANCE AND THE HUMAN SERVICES

By

CHARLES WOLFSON, M.S.W.

Professor of Social Work
University of Michigan
Ann Arbor, Michigan

CHARLES C THOMAS • PUBLISHER
Springfield • Illinois • U.S.A.

Published and Distributed Throughout the World by

CHARLES C THOMAS • PUBLISHER
2600 South First Street
Springfield, Illinois 62717

© *1984 by* **CHARLES C THOMAS • PUBLISHER**

ISBN 0-398-05005-8

Library of Congress Catalog Card Number: 84-3576

With **THOMAS BOOKS** *careful attention is given to all details of manufacturing and design. It is the Publisher's desire to present books that are satisfactory as to their physical qualities and artistic possibilities and appropriate for their particular use.* **THOMAS BOOKS** *will be true to those laws of quality that assure a good name and good will.*

Printed in the United States of America
SC–R-3

Library of Congress Cataloging in Publication Data

Wolfson, Charles.
    Social deviance and the human services.

    Bibliography: p.
    Includes index.
    1. Social work with the socially handicapped.
2. Deviant behavior—Labeling theory. 3. Social interaction. I. Title.
HV1568.W64   1984   362.8   84-3576
ISBN 0-398-05005-8

PREFACE

A number of years ago my attention was drawn to an incident that ordinarily would have had only passing significance. I accompanied a blind friend and colleague to a department store where he intended to purchase some minor items of clothing. The clerk who assisted us merely glanced at my friend and assumed that I was the sole customer, an error which I quickly corrected. This apparently made no difference to the clerk who directed questions to me about the size and color of the clothing at hand. When I firmly suggested that the clerk should direct these questions to my friend, her customer, something strange occurred. Now facing my friend but moving no closer, the clerk did exactly as I had requested but in a much louder tone of voice. Also, whenever my friend asked question in response to something the clerk had said, the clerk would turn to me as if appealing for help.

As it turned out this experience proved to be no more than a "normal" event in the life of a blind person, an ordinary interaction that illustrates how others react to blindness. What interested me about the incident, in which the clerk assumed, actually insisted upon, extraordinary dependency in her customer due to his disability, was her loud tone of voice when she finally addressed him. Did she believe him to be deaf as well as blind? When I mentioned this to my friend he indicated that this was a frequent occurrence, one to which he had become accustomed. What really annoyed him occurred quite often as he traveled around town by city bus. After being assisted onto the bus by another waiting passenger, his unacquainted helper would drop two tokens into the fare box, one for each of them, assuming that he was not only blind but destitute!

Such incidents hold considerable interest for the student of deviance theory because they contain elements of everyday life that are often overlooked due to their ordinariness. One element is just that, ordinary, minor interactions between people who are different in certain salient ways and others who take note of this difference. Another element is the predisposition of some actors who react to handicapped persons to be helpful, in their fashion. The department store clerk is trained to a role, performs it each workday and utilizes learned interactional tactics to facilitate customer satisfaction. The bus rider–helper reacts spontaneously with charitable intent; he could have easily ignored the blind man at the bus stop.

A third element common to these two incidents is the reactors' assumptions regarding associated disabilities, the linking of blindness with deafness in one case and poverty in the other. Were these ordinary people interacting with my friend who happens to be blind (but is neither deaf nor poor), or were they individuals playing out vignettes composed of stereotypes? Did they really see my friend or was it a stereotypic image of a blind man that they saw? The common phenomenon of observers linking varying conditions or disabilities is called deviance multiplication. Deaf persons are assumed to also be stupid, while retarded persons are assumed to be hard of hearing and homosexuals are thought to be prone to pederasty.

The phenomenon of deviance multiplication suggests that reactors do not see the person first because their attention is drawn to the disability; it is the differentness that is initially observed. Then, unconsciously, reactors conjure up an a priori established imagery in their minds that channels their reactions. This happens with ordinary people and with professionals who work with deviants in human service organizations. In addition, as we shall see, certain operations and features of human service organizations are grounded in these stereotypes. They erect ideologies and images about their clientele that serve to simplify reality and facilitate smooth running operations.

In recent years a large body of literature on the sociology of deviant behavior has been produced ranging from sophisticated theoretical statements to collections of descriptive material about how such deviant types as prostitutes and delinquents get by.

Much of this work is exciting because it shows the sociologist at his best in explaining the individual and society by seeking to understand the former and criticize the latter. It is through this work that sociologists present a social construction of reality, one in which the consequences of controlling human conduct are revealed. The material examined, men and society, is a traditional focus for sociologists but here the socially constrained consists of the marginal, the disabled, the rejected. Persons who are responsible for the identification and management of deviants, at times variously treat, persuade, control and change them by dint of their employment in human service organizations. They are the social workers, nurses, doctors, psychologists and psychiatrists who work in clinics, medical centers, mental hospitals, welfare agencies, public schools and courts throughout the country.

The study of deviance for the sociologist is an intellectual pursuit, while for the human service professional it is a vital undertaking intimately related to one's life work and consequent social perspectives. However, by and large, human service professionals are uninformed about the sociology of deviant behavior. Those few who do have a familiarity with the study of deviance perceive it as being unduly critical of their work and workplace.

This book is written for the future human service professional, for the student who seeks to make a career out of helping other people. It explicates the various theories of social deviance, examines explanatory models and draws linkages to social action. It is meant to be a translation of what the sociologists have been telling us but takes the next step by identifying the consequences of certain practices within the field of human service that exacerbate rather than reform problems of deviance.

This book is written for the student who sees deviance not as titillating facts about the underside of life but as central to the human condition. The study of deviance has direct and significant implications for developing an ideology and approach to clients that can be ameliorative, nurturing, and, in the end, truly helpful.

CONTENTS

SOCIAL DEVIANCE AND THE HUMAN SERVICES

Chapter 1

DEFINITIONS OF DEVIANCE

THE SUBJECTIVE SIDE OF DEVIANCE

Being required to define social deviance is a bit like having to answer the question "Is divorce good or bad?" We can answer only with another question, "From whose point of view?" We would also like to learn from the questioner if the answer should refer to the welfare of society, men, women, children, the church, or the long-term effects of divorce on each of these? If we were to undertake research to find answers to the question, should the study involve divorced men or divorced women or children whose parents are divorced? Should conclusions be published on the basis of a contemporary survey or should we wait twenty years while the children involved grow up? If we do wait, we might learn something about the long-term consequences of divorce on children instead of only its immediate effects.

In the end we might also say that we really cannot study families where there has been divorce unless we also consider non-divorced families for comparison. Even were we to find some differences, let us say, that boys and girls from divorced families are less secure at all ages than other children; are the differences the result of divorce? It could be that insecurity in children of divorced parents is the result of economic hardship and dislocation, factors that are related to but not necessarily caused by divorce.

There are a number of parallels between our hypothetical study of divorce and exploration of the concept, social deviance. At one time divorce was considered to be deviant by most people and that feeling continues today among certain groups. In addition, if we were to study deviants but not nondeviants, we would learn very little. Reversing the questions might lead to more productive answers. For example, we could ask, "Why do couples remain married and why do people conform?" We could also turn things completely around and wonder, "Why do you ask?" What images come to mind when you think about divorce? What images come to mind when you think about deviants? Where did you get these images, and what effect do you think they will have should you interact with a divorced woman or a deviant man?

Our point is that deviance is a subjective state although we are accustomed to thinking of it otherwise. We prefer to think of our world as orderly and attribute a special value to conformity. At times, when we see disorder and nonconformity, it is upsetting and makes us uncomfortable. By naming some behavior as deviance and some persons as deviant, we resolve certain problems. The act of naming provides an explanation, however superficial, for the existence of the deviant behavior. "Why do some people engage in illegal behavior? Because they are criminals, that's why!" "Why is that woman behaving so strangely in a public place? She must be mentally ill." In addition to offering explanations, naming deviants assists us in organizing our own reactions to them, particularly within interpersonal situations. By naming specific persons as deviants, we permit ourselves to violate rules of decorum and polite interaction; we can ignore or reject those who make us uncomfortable without feeling guilty. Each of these problems could not be so easily resolved if we did not think that deviance is an objective state that exists whether or not we observe and react to it.

Our own views about deviance reflect, to a considerable extent, our personal likes and dislikes. Our personal reactions to deviance, despite what we may choose to think, are not spontaneous and unique. We are socialized in ways that ultimately shape prescribed and learned responses to the characteristics and behaviors of others. The process of socialization, for the most part, is so smooth and natural that we do not bother to examine where we obtained one perspective or another.

The admonitions that we receive as children revolve around the issue of good versus bad. Bad boys steal candy, light fires in fields or vacant lots and play with their penises. Bad girls get dirty, tease other children and lie to their parents and teachers. The problem is that many of these acts of "badness" are pleasurable or serve to avoid punishment. The admonitions are then reinforced by adults with the addition of dire images. "you will grow up to become a liar and a cheat," or "a crook, thief, or crazy person." It is from such interactions that we learn to avoid engaging in prohibited behaviors and begin to develop negative reactions to those who are perceived to have engaged in them.

Daniel Glaser points out that most sociologists would define deviance as "any behavior or attribute for which an individual is regarded as objectionable in a particular social system."[1] Social systems, however, vary enormously in terms of which behaviors are regarded as being deviant, as can be seen from the following story.

> An old tale from the Orient concerns a man, far from home, who is traveling by horseback through the countryside of a strange land. It is evening and a full moon lights the road in front of him. As he approaches a small wooden bridge stretched over a stream, he sees a young woman wearing a long white gown standing by the water's edge. Now curious, he reins his horse to a halt and watches the woman. She is facing away from him, but this doesn't prevent him from hearing her plaintive sobbing. Touched, he alights from the horse and slowly approaches her.
>
> At the sound of his footsteps she turns toward him revealing her face. It is virtually featureless, lacking a nose, cheekbones, forehead, and chin protuberance; it is a blank white screen with tiny apertures for the mouth and eyes. Stifling his feelings of horror he attempts to console her, for he is convinced her weeping is caused by rejection as a result of her hideous deformity. At that moment a large number of people emerge from the partial darkness, completely surrounding the man and the young woman. He notes with mounting fear that all the people have featureless faces.

In our story the traveler, far from home, carries with him definitions and expectations from one social system as he enters another one. In applying these definitions to the young woman, alone and sobbing, he may assume that she is contemplating drowning herself in the nearby stream because of her deformity. In an instant the entire situation is reversed. None of the traveler's assumptions are correct, and he becomes the deviant.

The story demonstrates how our thoughts about deviances are bound by a culture that sets up expectations about how people should appear. When a person's appearance is at extreme variance from our expectations, we make assumptions about the nature of the person's feelings. We don't bother to question why we are having these thoughts; they seem natural to us. Such thoughts, in our view, are actually little theories that we carry around in our heads. The presence of these theories attests to the subjectivity involved in reaching our own culture-bound definitions of deviance. Deviance, therefore, is not an inherent attribute of any behavior; it is a theory that people hold about the behavior.[2] The fact that most people might agree that a certain behavior is deviant does not attest to its being an objective state. Such agreement only confirms that a particular theory is very pervasive. Even if most people believed in astrology, that would not necessarily make it true.

Deviance connotes a broad, mixed, vaguely-and-situationally-defined fluctuating assortment of conduct and characteristics.[3] The term is applied to so many different behaviors and characteristics that it defies any universal definition that might be attempted. It will be more productive, at least at this point, to view the concept of deviance as a loose assortment of theories that are held about selected behaviors or characteristics of some people by social audiences. I will explore distinctive aspects of deviance, as opposed to conformity, with reference to deviance as a negative act or characteristic attributed to some persons by others. In turn these persons fill deviant statuses that are ultimately defined and used by organizations that are established to do something about deviants.

ELEMENTS USEFUL IN UNDERSTANDING DEVIANCE

1. Deviance as a Negative Quality

Deviance and conformity are necessarily linked together; each implies the existence of the other. Good cannot exist without reference to evil, its opposite. As Jack D. Douglas has noted: "It is this categorical distinction which lies behind the dichotomizing of the social world into morally disjunct categories—right side of the tracks versus wrong side of the tracks, criminal versus noncriminal, ... respectable versus disreputable, evil versus good, black versus white, and so on."[4] Deviance, as an attributed designation is always intended to be negative. In order for an act to be designated deviant, some significant audience must view it as negative behavior.

Cigarette smoking, particularly in public places, is increasingly becoming a deviant act. Many persons find the behavior disagreeable; local ordinances prohibit smoking in various public places; governmental and private agencies advertise denouncing it; and treatment-oriented classes to eliminate the habit are advertised in newspapers throughout the country. The nondeviant way is epitomized by reference to those who have never smoked, those who have stopped smoking, and those who don't smoke in public.

Negative interpretations are made about the deviant behavior as well as the persons engaged in the behavior. Deviant behavior is seen frequently as a threat to the common good, as behavior that is harmful to others, either in actuality or symbolically. Other behaviors that are considered to be deviant are acts that are not only disagreeable but are presumed to be harmful to the nonconforming person. Being excessively overweight elicits responses from audiences such as "disgusting" and "how can anyone do that to their body?" Another type of deviant behavior is initiated by people who harm neither others nor themselves but contest symbolic norms and beliefs, such as those who refuse to stand for the playing of the national anthem or fail to recite the pledge of allegiance at public events.

These judgements that people make about other people are negative ones; the behavior or condition is considered undesirable. Those who engage in the behavior, the deviants, are generally held to be at least partially, if not fully, responsible for their actions.

2. Deviance and Deviant Persons

A simple and direct tautology would tell us that deviance is that behavior in which deviant persons engage. There is a considerable difference, however, between identifying acts as negative and disapproving of them and naming persons engaged in these behaviors as deviants. Deviants engage in conforming behavior most of the time, and all of us engage in deviant behavior some of the time. Picking one's nose, loud belching, and masturbation are behaviors that, when done in private, receive little or no condemnation. Acts of minor shoplifting; finding money and not turning it in to authorities; or taking home small parts from the shop or paper and pencils from the office are things that most people do or have done at some time in their lives. For most acts of deviance there is no deviant because the individual's behavior is not known or the behavior is normalized by the person's reference group.

Another cluster of behaviors that may violate conventions is observed by others but explained away by such words as, "I didn't know what I was doing" or "I was really upset when I did that." In addition, intimate audiences frequently issue unsolicited excuses such as "That's not like her" or "He's really under a lot of pressure." Essentially, these are integrative statements that excuse the person violating the convention and assert, in the face of contradictory evidence, the basic normality of the rule breaker.

To unite the deviant actor with the deviant act requires an attribution that extends both into the nature of the deviance being observed and beyond it to determinations about the kind of person who would do that sort of thing. He or she is said to have problems of character; either it is deficient or poorly shaped. That person is not like the rest of us. In this way the deviance becomes both magnified and personalized, the embodying of evil and differentness. For example, consider the hypothetical case of a man driving his car on the highway. Suddenly the car veers sharply to the left, crosses the median and hits an oncoming auto. Our driver is slightly injured; the four occupants in the car that was struck are severely injured. An act of deviance has taken place; reckless driving resulting in an accident and injuries to innocent people.

Suppose that we vary the reason for the accident's occurrence. In scenario one, the driver has a heart attack, blacks out, and loses control of his car. Causation is determined but fault is not attributed to the man personally. In scenario two, the man is drunk and as a consequence is unable to control his car. Fault is found and is attributed to him. He draws legal penalties, feels guilty about what he has done, and is seen by others as being weak-willed, irresponsible, and dangerous.

The second scenario unites deviance and the deviant through a motivational chain. The man had choices; the heart attack victim did not, in this view. It is in such ways that observers attribute to the person characteristics not shared by the rest of us.

3. Deviant Behavior and Deviant Attributes

Throughout this discussion we have referred to deviant behavior and deviant persons. We might also suggest that there is no necessary connection between the two; for indeed, an innocent man may be imprisoned or a sane woman may be institutionalized in a mental hospital. The popular view is that they have been properly incarcerated and can therefore be identified and treated as deviants. Some persons become deviant without reference to any particular behavior on their part. The very ugly, the overly tall, and the dwarf possess physical characteristics that are observed to vary widely from the norm. While persons with one or another of these characteristics frequently make successful adjustments, they tend to be objects of ridicule and rejection during periods in their lives. Thomas Wolfe, the novelist, recounts the pain and strangeness he felt as a youth who was six feet seven inches tall before basketball became popular.[5]

Still another group of persons is inferred to be deviant because of their personal physical configuration such as the overweight. Deviance, in this case, is attributed to gluttony or lack of self-discipline. The behavior of overeating does not need to be observed by audiences since the effects of the assumed deviance are visible to all.

Many sociologists point out that there is a clear differentiation between deviant behavior and conditions or states such as physical handicaps, tics, and facial disfigurements. Albert K. Cohen suggests a qualitative difference exists between the two in the following passage:

> Involuntary physical and mental states are regarded as socially disvalued roles but are they deviant? The role of slave, hunchback, moron, sick person, and the blind are disvalued but socially they are felt to be different from such roles as coward, thief, scab, or adulterer. What the latter have in common is the notion of a person who knows what he is doing and is capable of doing otherwise, but who chooses to violate some normative rule, and so may be held to account for this behavior. By contrast, the element of choice is absent from the physically impaired. There are disvalued roles that are unfortunate but not reprehensible.[6]

Daniel Glaser, on the other hand, seems to argue the point before he concludes by agreeing with Cohen. Glaser notes various physical conditions such as being a midget or amputee; being spastic, blind, deaf, and dumb; or being of a minority racial group has led to such persons being treated "as objectionable in many communities, organizations, or other social systems" and in "terms of the reactions they arouse . . . they certainly have much similarity to other forms of deviance." But because these are conditions rather than acts they "cannot be called deviant behavior."[7]

Robert A. Scott, in writing about the treatment of the blind follows Glaser's point to its logical, although not intended conclusion. People who suffer from physical defects and others who appear to voluntarily violate conformity receive similar reactions from lay audiences and professionals in that they are seen as being morally inferior. Scott, in considering "mental illness, crime, delinquency, poverty, blindness, mental retardation, and alcoholism" as deviance, writes that "it is the fact of moral deviation which is common to all of them . . . that allows me to regard them as comparable phenomena."[8]

Since deviance is subjectively determined, inferential, and reliant upon the negative reactions of others, it is preferable to view both deviant conditions and behavior as being two sides of the same coin. While we may feel profoundly sorry for someone who has cancer and not consider that person as deviant, there are many others who do. Reports of persons being treated for cancer and their subsequent inability to find employment, loss of friends, and increasing involuntary isolation appear regularly in newspapers throughout the United States. The sick role is a deviant state, as Talcott Parsons has pointed out, because of its threat to the stability of the social system through impaired role performance. The difference between illness and, for example, crime is that the former is not seen as willful deviance.[9] Illness is somewhat less of a moral failing than is criminal behavior, but illness remains a problem of morality when chronicity leads to dependency in a society in which everyone is supposed to "pull their own weight."

4. Deviant Statuses

Perhaps the confusion between deviant behavior and deviant attributes may best be clarified by reference to how people are categorized in our society. One way that people judge others is with reference to statuses. Statuses, in the United States, are ordinarily arranged according to occupation. Judges and auto workers are in occupations that earn them a particular status, and this is said to be their master status. People usually associate irrelevant characteristics with master statuses that serves to fill out a complete picture in their minds. These are called auxiliary traits whereby judges are assumed to be male, white, and middle-aged or older. People tend to be surprised when they meet or see judges who are black or young or female.

Another type of master status is that granted to people when they are placed in one or another deviant category. The transformation from normal to deviant character reflects a marked change in status. The student who is "slow" in performing his school work may also be seen as tall, cooperative, friendly, and easily frustrated by both peers and teachers, but he is still one pupil among many. Should he be formally designated as retarded by school officials, a chain of events will begin that transforms him into becoming a very different sort of pupil. If he is placed in a special classroom along with other retarded pupils, it is likely that his subsequent reputation from this act alone will make him appear to be a new person among peers and neighbors. What had been an "auxiliary status," slow student, has now become a "master status," retarded person.

The utility of status categories is that they provide instant recognition. This facilitates our understanding about other people in our world and what they do. We hold images, however superficial and inaccurate, about what engineers do and what teachers are like. We also hold images about deviants. Deviant statuses, such as the mentally ill, the criminal, or the physically handicapped, tend to be seen as master statuses with a range of interconnected, negative traits. The person is first and foremost a deviant, assumed to be unpredictable and potentially violent if mentally ill, untrustworthy and calculating if criminal, and dependent if physically handicapped. When exceptions are discovered, such as handicapped persons climbing a mountain, our images may be revised but it is unlikely that they are eliminated.

While status categories provide a useful function in enabling people to recognize others without reconstructing their entire background, they also serve to separate persons from one another. When people are moved into deviant statuses, other human qualities are discounted or seem to disappear. Criminals are not thought of as being fathers or mothers; drug users do not have occupations; and prostitutes don't play bridge. It is these shared qualities in people that encourage identification. In their absence deviants are seen as people who are truly different.

5. Definition by Organizations

Public reactions to deviant behavior are generally expressive rather than active. People become upset when they view or learn about certain behaviors. They may display emotional reactions, such as anger and fear, but they rarely act directly to confront the deviant or to "stamp out" the deviance. At times, public reaction is channeled into political activity by moral entrepreneurs in an effort to persuade civic and governmental leaders to take action against deviants. This was true of Anita Bryant, an entertainer and born-again Christian, who led a successful fight in Dade County, Florida, to repeal an ordinance barring discrimination against homosexuals in employment, housing, and public accommodations. Bryant's group attempted to influence elected and appointed officials of local government to implement policies permitting discrimination against homosexuals. However, even such entrepreneurial activities as Bryant's tend to involve only a small number of people in a highly publicized effort. Furthermore, their activities are directed at influencing other organizations and governmental units into taking actions the entrepreneurs see as desirable.

It has only been within the past twenty years that attention has been drawn to specific organizations as deviance defining bodies. The sociologist, Edwin Lemert, expanded the area for studying deviance when he wrote:

A sociological theory of deviance must focus specifically on the interactions which not only define the behavior as deviant but also organize and activate the application of sanctions by individuals, groups and agencies. ... [T]he socially significant differentiation of deviants from non-deviants is increasingly contingent upon circumstances of situatioh, place, social and personal biography and bureaucratically organized agencies of social control.[10]

What is it that these organizations do with regard to deviance? Institutions and agents of social control have been given the responsibility of defining, minimizing, eliminating, or normalizing deviant behavior.[11]

Organizations typically thought of as deviance defining institutions include police agencies, courts, and mental hospitals. Other organizations that are not usually thought of in this regard expend a considerable amount of their resources in defining deviance. They include, among others, public child protection agencies (child abuse), community mental health centers (mental illness), various organizations serving the blind (legal blindness) and physically handicapped (permanently disabled), as well as the public school (emotionally impaired, educably retarded). It is to these organizations that the allocation of authority and power to define deviance has been accorded.

Many people believe that deviance inheres entirely in the behavior of individuals. Strange and unusual people are deviant. What the eyes see is the only reality. These beliefs tend to ignore the role of power and authority in society. Power involves the ability to have a particular set of definitions of behavior realized and to the extent that such definitions receive general support authority can be transacted. However, simpler views prevail. When college students are asked "What is a juvenile delinquent?" they usually respond by stating, "A youth who has broken the law." When a list of offenses contained in the state juvenile code is distributed, it is discovered that at one time or another every student in the classroom has "broken the law." The answers to the question "What is mental illness?" provided by these same students tends to be more varied but follow the same logic. It is assumed that precise definitions exist and that the mental illness designation accurately reflects the qualities of a person. Students defined mentally ill persons as "someone who acts in a bizarre manner" or "people with deep-seated problems." Again, each student acknowledged that at one time or another, he or she fit that description.

The students' treatment of deviance in these examples reflects an opinion that deviance consists of distinctive categories that are neatly arranged. One category is established for one set of phenomena, another for a different set. The categories of deviance, in this view, are somewhat like the organization of knowledge in universities. Geometry is what is taught in a "math" class, governmental operations is the subject of a political science class. What is true in the university however, with its orderly division of knowledge, is not true of the manner in which deviance is determined.

In fact, it is the juvenile court that determines whether or not delinquency is a fact, and this determination can be made only about youth brought before the court. Many youths who engage in delinquent behavior may escape detection while others may not be labeled delinquents because their parents agree to plan for referral to a psychiatrist in private practice. Similarly, only certain organizations possess the power and authority to define people as mentally ill. In our society it is the courts, psychiatrists, community mental health centers, and mental hospitals that are empowered to do this. Prior to organizational action, we have opinions about who may be delinquent and who may be mentally ill. Organizations, by confirming or denying these opinions create the facts for us.

It should be noted, however, that for the most part human service organizations define who is deviant rather than what is deviance. There is a vast difference between proclaiming undesirable behavior as deviance and naming someone as being deviant. In identifying someone as deviant, that individual is placed into an existing category that is widely recognized. The definition of the category precedes the act of placement. Identifying acts as deviance is a political process involving the exercise of power. Special interest groups, such as the one mobilized by Anita Bryant, attempt to have their definitions of deviance accepted. It is left to specific organizations to decide who is and is not deviant.

No single organization is established to deal with the universe of deviant acts. They tend to specialize, that is, organizations deal with categories of deviance. Different organizations define who is mentally ill, who is a criminal, and who is alcoholic.

These organizations are not solely repositories of expert knowledge and skill in defining deviance but consist of intricate processes in which humans make errors, demonstrate biases, and behave politically. At times and for various reasons, organizations perform their deviant defining task crudely and err by defining a person who is engaged in nonconforming behavior as meeting the requirements of a deviant category.

Organizations that are specifically mandated with the responsibility of sifting out deviants from nondeviants will mistakenly envelop within their definitions and processes significant numbers of people who are actually normal but fall just within or near the category for which the organization is responsible. For example, in her study of the public schools' determination of mental retardation in a community in California, Jane Mercer found that the over-representation of Mexican-American children in classes for the retarded was as great as four and a half times more than what would be expected based on the proportion of these children in the population. When the author utilized a "two-dimensional definition of mental retardation rather than almost exclusive reliance on I.Q. test scores which the school district preferred," she found that 75 percent of the children identified as retarded were mislabeled. That is, these children met no other criteria for the retardation label other than low scores on IQ tests. They were not seen as being retarded by their families, peers, or even other agencies in the community.[12]

If the deviance is incorrectly ascribed, does this make the person any the less deviant? Apparently not, if it is an organization that is doing the ascribing. Usually the consequences of a false designation are not very different from those that occur in the lives of individuals that do actually engage in deviant acts. Robert K. Merton, in discussing the self-fulfilling prophecy notes, "Men respond not only to the objective features of a situation, but also, and at times primarily, to the meaning this situation has for them. And once they have assigned some meaning to the situation, their consequent behavior and some of the consequences of that behavior are determined by the ascribed meaning."[13]

People tend to have diffuse, stereotypic ideas about what deviance is and what deviants are like. Organizations help to clarify the matter by making official determinations of who the deviants are. In a sense, however, organizations are simply social groups that have been invested with authority in certain matters. Organizations do not act; people act. Shortly, we shall turn to the people who engage in the social mandate of defining deviants.

The five elements useful in understanding deviance that have been described imply that defining deviance can be a complicated matter. Our definition must take some account of both the person and society as well as shifting patterns of what is designated as deviance over time. John I. Kitsuse has provided a definition that meets these requirements. He defines deviance as a process by "which the members of a group, community or society 1) interpret behavior as deviant; 2) define persons who so behave as a certain kind of deviant; and 3) accord the treatment considered appropriate to such deviants."[14]

DEFINITIONS OF DEVIANCE BY PROFESSIONALS

One way to objectify an object or an act is to define it. Reality is imparted to objects and behavior through definitions. The power to define objects and behavior is not located haphazardly within the social structure of a society, but is accorded to dominant groups. Conrad and Schneider note that "During the Middle Ages and through the Inquisition, the Church had the authority and power to define activities as deviant. With the decline of the Church and subsequent secularization, the state increasingly gained authority to define deviance."[15] It has only been within the last 130 years or so that the state in industrialized societies has accorded professionals the responsibility for definition of deviance. Scott presents an optimistic picture of this development when he writes that—

> The view has emerged that helplessness and dependency are not inherent conditions that are stigmatizing (deviant), so that many such people are able to engage in productive social and economic activities if given help and training. Moreover, the existence of traits or qualities that stigmatize

is no longer explained by recourse to notions of moral culpability; rather, the deficiencies are seen as the product of ordinary genetic, psychological, social, and economic processes that operate in all societies. Along with these changes in the connotations associated with stigma, there has been a corresponding shift in the locus of responsibility for the education, rehabilitation, and care of people affiliated with them. This responsibility has been moving from the family to professionally trained people who claim to have a special expertise which uniquely qualifies them to understand and treat the problems associated with stigmatizing conditions. Many of these experts have trained in social work, rehabilitation counseling, work with the deaf, work with the blind, psychiatry and the various mental health professions. Moreover, a majority of them work in specialized helping organizations, most of which have become large, complex bureaucratic structures.[16]

The experts to whom Scott refers we shall term *human service professionals.* They are the personnel of human service organizations who define and attempt to rehabilitate deviants. Human service professionals generally consider themselves to be moral persons who, as a consequence of their work, contribute to the alleviation of pain and suffering and help make the world a better place in which to live. Many see themselves as sympathetic and solicitous to the deviant with whom they come into contact. Most prefer to refer to these troubled persons as clients or patients. The handling and managing of deviants is viewed as being in their own behalf or if not entirely so, then favoring some social good. A professional ideology (shared understandings and beliefs) explains the world and the human services professional's role in it, as well as the role of the client. It is a special view of life and events that is more extensive than an official code of ethics or a profession's creed.[17]

Geoffrey Pearson, referring to social work, indicates that its representation of itself to itself is the emphatic embrace of "human subjectivity and . . . a carrier of the human tradition of compassion." Professional principles indicate that one should "start where the client is," treat him as an "individual" and pay attention to his "needs" while accepting him in a nonjudgemental manner, regardless of his faults.[18]

The public's view of deviants as people who are starkly different is rejected in the professional ideology in favor of a more accepting and universal one. In this view the distinction between deviants and nondeviants is assumed to be minor and transitory if the individual seeks and receives help from professional sources. Slogans are heard such as "mental illness is an illness just like any other" and "it takes strength to ask for help." These slogans fly in the face of popular beliefs and imply that only minor degrees of difference exist between deviants and nondeviants.

A professional ideology consists of abstract generalizations that represent the profession to itself and part of the public. It is made up of ideas that rely on symbolism rather than articulation of techniques. Regardless, the ideology is intended to guide the application of technique as in the physician's proscription, "Do no harm!"

Scott points out that there is another side to professional ideology, namely a specialized body of knowledge that has been acquired through careful professional training and/or years of clinical experiences. "As a rule this knowledge is codified into theories about particular conditions such as mental illness, blindness, deafness, poverty, and so on. These theories contain general assertions about the nature of human behavior, its causes, and how to change it."[19] It is within these theories that we find definitions of deviance. Such definitions, however, are only partly determined by professional training, exposure to scientific studies of deviants, and direct experience. "Their content is also determined by, and reflects, certain social, cultural, and political forces in the environment in which (professional) experts are immersed. . . ."[20]

KEY COMPONENTS OF PROFESSIONALS' DEFINITIONS

Since deviance is a subjective state, a product of the attributions of others, human service professionals are constrained by various existing definitions that the public holds. Professionals cannot redefine and claim, for example, that convicts should be freed immediately since the acts that led to their incarceration were no less than the revolutionary strivings of an underclass consisting of exploited and downtrodden people. They also cannot claim that the large number of public school pupils who engage in maladaptive behavior are simply responding to oppressive school regimes and associated overregimentation.

There is a range of existing definitions of social problems and deviant behavior that is generally accepted within a society of which professionals must be aware and within which they must operate. Robert D. Vinter identifies the source of these public definitions:

> The degree of (perceived) jeopardy for others, the age and sex of the deviant, and the normative areas in which behavior violates expectations are among the conditions that shape public response to the deviancy. In an important sense, however, the many forms of deviance are perceived as alike. . . . [F]ulfillment of conventional roles tends to be regarded as the responsibility of the individual. Conformity and deviance, like success and failure, are seen as matters of personal volition and as somehow inhering in the character and willfulness of each individual. . . . Persisting belief that the deviant intentionally violates expectations produces a continuous strain toward punitive and exclusionary measures and a reluctance to allocate generous resources in support of the treatment organization. . . . [T]hese elements in belief and valuation serve to define the essential nature of the client populations and the mandates for change.[21]

In addition, human service organizations that employ professionals are mandated to serve specific client populations who present delimited attributes and conditions, that is, they tend to specialize in certain types of deviance definition and control.

Nevertheless, human service professionals and their organizations are in a position to influence as well as be influenced by public definitions of deviance. Public definitions tend to be overly general, diffuse, and nonspecific. While they may present parameters within which action can occur, they cannot serve as guidelines for action. Public definitions of truly "unworthy" deviants, for example, criminals, would warrant against building swimming pools in prisons as well as for regularly beating prisoners with truncheons. Somewhere between these polarized extremes, prison psychologists and counselors are free to act on and in behalf of inmates.

There are four components of human service professionals' definitions of deviance that we intend to identify. They are posed as being linked rather than mutually exclusive.

(1) Problems of deviance are held to be basically individual in character. The underlying assumption is that the problem is located within

the individual. This view does not necessarily ignore the impact of social factors in causing and sustaining deviance; indeed, such forces are seen as exacerbating already weakened personal conditions. While economic recession may promote an increase in crime and mental illness, most people succumb to neither. The inadequacy or condition "belongs" to the person, not the socioeconomic structure of society. Furthermore, human service professionals, as a consequence of the way services are organized, have face-to-face contact with deviants and are in a position to manipulate individuals and not the economy, legislation, or slums. Organizational arrangements in which human service professionals work dictate a case-by-case or individual-by-individual approach.

(2) Problems of deviance are reducible to matters of psychology. Traditionally, human service professionals have drawn heavily on psychological theory to explain human problems or dysfunction, with diagnostic categories of the American Psychiatric Association being a major tool in conceptualizations.[22] Those organizations and services that do not utilize a psychiatric nomenclature rely nevertheless upon perspectives derived from psychodynamic and/or learning theory. Even in the case of rehabilitation of the blind, as Scott reports, workers "espouse many different theories about blindness. Most of these theories are cast in psychological terms. In them, the focus is on the impact which blindness is thought to have on personality and psychological adjustment."[23]

(3) Psychological problems are virtually universal. The reductionism involved in defining certain types of deviance as being essentially psychological in character encourages the application of similar definitions to all deviance. Human service professionals claim a psychological expertise that is of use in treating not only the mentally ill and the criminal but also includes the blind, the poverty-stricken, the malperforming public school pupil, the retarded, the physically ill, and the aged. Furthermore, the knowledge and techniques derived from psychology can be extended to prevent breakdowns from occurring in the normal but beset individual who is troubled by marital disharmony, periods of depression, annoying habits, unsatisfactory sexual performance, and unsuccessful child rearing practices. At times, it seems that the domain claimed by

human service professionals omits no aspect of human behavior.

There is a close interaction between human service professionals and their organizations in what appears to be a type of imperialist expansionism. As social problems are defined, such as child or spouse abuse, parent abuse in the case of the elderly, or failure to thrive among infants, entrepreneurial interests within the professions claim that the problem falls within their domain and simultaneously cite it as being of epidemic proportions. Such utterances and claims are at the heart of deviance definitions because they direct attention to behaviors for which there is little public recognition and agreement.

(4) The ultimate goal of deviance definition is power. The success of the definitional process is decided by who has the power to legitimate their definitions.[24] This does not mean to imply that power cannot be exercised for humane purposes or that human service organizations and professionals dabble in power for devious reasons. However, I am suggesting that the realization of power improves the status and well-being of a profession and its members. Power possessed by a profession increases its autonomy, allows for self-regulation rather than external regulation, and permits professional definitions and decisions to go unchallenged. Many years ago, E. M. Jellinek expressed the value of power in arriving at a contested definition of alcoholism most succinctly when he wrote: "Physicians know what belongs in their realm. . . . a disease is what the medical profession recognizes as such, whether a part of the public likes it or not, and even if a minority of the medical profession is disinclined to accept the idea."[25]

Human service professionals are aware of the power enjoyed by the physician and the ease by which the medical profession has its definitions accepted by the public. Clearly, medicine is a dominant profession, and the physician is autonomous or self-directing in his work.[26] To make decisions that are noncontrovertible can be enviable, especially to the human service professional who must rely upon persuasion as his or her major technique.

The ability of a profession to make claims and have them realized leads to increased power and an enlarged domain, despite the uncertainties and unknowns in the field. Robert A. Woodruff and others identify the domain to which psychiatrists wish to lay stake:

> Any condition associated with discomfort, pain, disability, death, or an *increased liability* to these states, regarded by physicians and the public as properly the responsibility of the medical profession, may be considered a disease. Whether a condition is regarded as a disease is a function of many factors: social, economic, biological, etc. As a society becomes better educated and more secular, disabilities often cease to be regarded as moral or theological problems and become medical ones.[27] (Italics added.)

The extension of the definition of disease to include all "personal, social, and ethical problems in living" has been vigorously criticized by Thomas D. Szasz but continues today unabated.[28] In attempting to unite mood states and discomfort with disease, psychiatry lays claim to an unlimited range of human behavior and conditions.

To recapitulate, we are proposing that one goal of the human service professions is the attainment of power with professional dominance as the desired state. The model that is pursued is that of the medical profession.

THE RELATIONSHIP BETWEEN DEFINITIONS AND ACTION

We have proposed that one consequence of defining deviance as an attribute or behavior of a person is to focus professional effort on bringing about individual change. In the case of child abuse, for example, the human service professional is preoccupied with incidents of this behavior within the immediate family constellation. Such problems as poverty, inadequate public assistance grants, poor childhood nutrition, deteriorating inner city schools, and other related public health issues will be ignored except as they occur in a specific case. Therefore, case intervention can never redress significant social problems.

In addition, increased probability of mistreatment of children can be located in the very organizations in which professionals function. The mass handling of children in public schools, juvenile court detention facilities, residential institutions, and training schools offers considerable potential for child abuse. In some of these locations, children are punished by being struck with paddles, deprived of food, forcibly restrained, locked in a room for days, or denied a number of basic freedoms. These actions may be recognized by human service professionals as disagreeable but rarely enter into their definitions of child abuse. The focus of the professional's action, therefore, based upon his or her definitions and claimed expertise is severely limited and is likely to be directed at achieving change in the abusing parent or caretakers.

Within this framework of individualizing problems of deviance, however, a multiplicity of definitions still exists. There is considerable variation in professionals' "assumptions about the causes and cures of deviance, how much of what kind of change is possible, and how to achieve this change."[29] Within the field of delinquency control, for example, there is the view expressed in such programs as "Scared Straight" that delinquents are both naive and willful actors who can be shocked out of their devious ways. At the other end of the spectrum are professionals who offer long-term, intensive, individual psychotherapy as the only effective answer to problems of delinquency. The definitions or interpretation about what caused the delinquent behavior and what needs to be done to the youth to correct it are at considerable odds, as are the prescribed treatments. Furthermore, the various professionals engaged in providing these disparate treatments are undoubtedly convinced that the one each has chosen is effective and that the others are not.

Definitions of deviance held by professionals and others are intimately linked to an identification of what the problem is, who has it, what should be done about it, and what types of policies are needed to reduce its occurrence. Commenting on alcoholism, for example, David J. Armor and others, identify the significance of definitions at all levels of the problem. To quote Armor, "Epidemological studies ... hinge on the criterion used for nose counting; treatment is limited to those individuals diagnosed as alcoholics. The prevailing medical definition of the 'effect' in question determines the search for relevant causal links and public policy toward treatment and prevention is influenced by the scope of the defined problem."[30]

If alcoholism is defined as a disease, then the medical profession is seen as the legitimate agent of social control.[31] If most forms of deviance can be defined as behavioral and emotional problems of people, then the human service professions are the legitimate agents for that turf.

REFERENCES

1. Daniel Glaser, *Social Deviance* (Chicago: Markham Publishing Company, 1971) p. 1.
2. S. Kirson Weinberg, "Disordered Behavior and Socially Deviant Behavior," in *The Sociology of Mental Disorders*, ed. S. Kirson Weinberg (Chicago: Aldine Publishing Company, 1967) p. 166.
3. Glaser, *Social Deviance*, p. 2.
4. Jack D. Douglas, ed., *Deviance and Respectability: The Social Construction of Moral Meanings*, (New York: Basic Books, 1970) p. 5.
5. Thomas Wolfe, *Of Time and The River* (Garden City, New York: The Dial Press, 1944).
6. Albert K. Cohen, *Deviance and Control* (Englewood Cliffs, New Jersey: Prentice-Hall, Inc., 1966) p. 36.
7. Glaser, *Social Deviance*, p. 21.
8. Robert A. Scott, "The Construction of Conceptions of Stigma by Professional Experts," in *Deviance and Respectability*, ed. Douglas, p. 258.
9. Talcott Parsons, *The Social System* (New York: The Free Press, 1951) pp. 428–29.
10. Edwin Lemert, *Human Deviance, Social Problems, and Social Control*, 2nd ed. (Englewood Cliffs, N.J.: Prentice-Hall, 1972) p. 18.
11. Peter Conrad and Joseph W. Schneider, *Deviance and Medicalization* (St. Louis, Missouri: The C. V. Mosby Company, 1980) p. 8.
12. Jane Mercer, "Institutionalized Anglocentrism: Labeling Mental Retardates in the Public Schools," *Race, Change and Urban Society, 5:* 311–338, 1971
13. Robert K. Merton, *Social Theory and Social Structure* (Glencoe: The Free Press, 1962) pp. 421–422.
14. John I. Kitsuse, "Societal Reaction to Deviant Behavior: Problems of Theory and Method," *Social Problems, 9* (Winter): 247–256, 1962.
15. Conrad and Schneider, *Deviance and Medicalization*, p. 8.
16. Scott, "Conceptions of Stigma," pp. 255–56.
17. Geoffrey Pearson, *The Deviant Imagination* (New York: Holmes and Meier Publishers, 1975) p. 128.
18. Pearson, *Deviant Imagination*, p. 128.
19. Scott, "Conceptions of Stigma," p. 257.
20. Scott, "Conceptions of Stigma," p. 269.
21. Robert D. Vinter, "Analysis of Treatment Organizations," in *Human Service Organizations*, eds. Yeheskel Hasenfeld and Richard A. English (Ann Arbor: The University of Michigan Press, 1974) p. 36.
22. Roger M. Nooe, "A Model for Integrating Theoretical Approaches to Deviance," *Social Work, 25* (5) (Sept. 1980): 366–70, 1980.
23. Scott, "Conceptions of Stigma," p. 260.

24. Conrad and Schneider, *Deviance and Medicalization*, p. 20.

25. E. M. Jellinek, *The Disease Concept of Alcoholism* (New Brunswick, New Jersey: Hillhouse Press, 1960) p. 12.

26. Eliot Freidson, "Dominant Professions, Bureaucracy, and Client Services," in *Human Service Organizations*, eds. Hasenfeld and English, pp. 428–448.

27. Robert A. Woodruff, Donald W. Goodwin, and Samuel B. Guze, *Psychiatric Diagnosis* (New York: Oxford University Press, 1974) p. 185.

28. Thomas S. Szasz, *The Myth of Mental Illness* (New York: Hoeber-Harper, 1961), p. 296.

29. Vinter, "Treatment Organizations," p. 37.

30. David J. Armor, J. Michael Polich, and Harriet B. Stambul, *Alcoholism in Treatment* (Santa Monica, California: The Rand Corporation, 1976) p. 34.

31. Conrad and Schneider, *Deviance and Medicalization*, p. 26.

Chapter 2

ETIOLOGIES OF DEVIANCE
Psychological Views

SELECTING A THEORY

All attempts to explain behavior, deviant or otherwise, involve reference to something about the actor—the structure of his personality, his perspectives, values, goals, interests, temperament, needs, drives—and something about the situation in which he acts."[1] The particular feature about the actor or his situation selected for emphasis as an explanatory variable involves the observer in theory selection.

Many human service professionals share the conviction, borrowed from medicine, that locating the causes of a disease or problem is a requisite for full and effective treatment. The practice of medicine, however, is supported by the sciences of chemistry and physics, which involve the use of established laboratory procedures in detecting causative agents for suspected conditions. Furthermore, both practice and procedure are usually instigated at the request of a complaining patient. The human service professional, on the other hand, frequently enters into another realm entirely, one characterized by layers of subjective judgement about people and events without the support of scientifically-based procedures.

Let us consider an example of a type of behavior that is nondeviant but undesirable from society's viewpoint. A recent news report informs us of federal government concern over the failure of many college students to repay guaranteed loans. The report indicates that the amount of default for one year alone, 1978, was $732 million. The report goes on to point out that this amount was more than four times greater than all the losses from robberies in the nation during the same year.

How shall we think about these facts? Is the problem within the student loan program or is it a problem of defaulting students? Is it a problem in the first place? We can decide that it is indeed a problem since it bears on governmental expenditures and, ultimately, how tax dollars are used or misused, a current matter of considerable public concern. If we focus on the student as the problem, how shall we think about this? We can take the position that the expenses involved in attending college are so onerous that some loan default is a logical expectation. Or, on the other hand, we can view the situation as a problem of morality that may eventually erode the fabric of society.

However we define the problem will do no more than point us toward a theory of causation. Should we determine, after extensive investigation, that loan-defaulting college students are different than other students in personality, social class background, and grade point average, we will not have moved a step closer to determining causes. In the first place, we assume that differences exist between these two groups of students and that these differences can be detected. Second, we assume that within these differences it is possible to locate factors that contribute to the motivation not to repay loans. Our assumptions are much too grandiose. The problem is, of course, that we need to approach our work, be it evaluating why some college students default or understanding what causes a person to behave in a certain way, with a theory in mind. Since we rarely have the inclination or time to fully examine each situation before developing generalizations or theoretical explanations, theories serve to reduce the complexity of phenomena that we observe or about which we hear and help to make them understandable. There are theories about why some people are attracted to certain types of persons and repelled by others. If we had to analyze each and every interpersonal situation "from scratch," the world would be a very confusing place indeed. The orientation of theory is to the analytic simplicity of the conceptual world; it serves to reduce and organize our thoughts. Theories are based ultimately on analytic concepts that are logically interrelated to help explain complex behavior.[2]

In their work, human service professionals draw upon a variety of theories that appear to offer explanations for certain aspects of human behavior. Certain aspects of a number of these theories will be explored as to how they relate to and illuminate deviant behavior, but a full exposition of any one will not be provided since this information can and should be obtained elsewhere. It is this author's intention to explore those elements of various theories that have particular relevance to the work of the human service professional.

PSYCHOLOGICAL THEORIES OF DEVIANCE CAUSATION

There are "countless theories and fragments of theories that fall under" the heading of psychology with this much in common: they seek to explain the difference in behavior between one person and another, or between the same person on two different days. Attempts that seek to understand and explain behavior with reference to "differences among persons, in the situations they face, and in the interactions between them we call psychological."[3] When we turn to psychological theories of deviant behavior, we focus on the actor side or "kinds of people theories," asking, "What sort of person would do this sort of thing?" followed by "How did they get this way?"[4] As Cohen notes, "The independent variable becomes some background event or circumstance, or pattern of events or circumstances, that, according to the theory, should produce such a personality."[5] That is, there is a tendency for people to attribute causality for their own behavior or that of others within their social group to temporary or transitional situational circumstances. The behavior in question is explained with reference to external pressures or stimuli. Human service professionals, however, will attempt to interpret client behavior as reflecting some quality of the actor. The attribution by the professional will tend to be personality-focused rather than situational. Behavior that may be seen by the client as common or infrequent or externally-provoked is regarded by the professional as truly revealing that individual's personal dispositions. The following overheard interchange between a social worker and a woman suspected of being schizophrenic may illustrate the point:

Client (sighing): I'm just not feeling myself today.
Social worker: No? Who do you think you are?
The focus on causation in many psychological theories inevi-

tably leads to a permeating concern on the part of the professional with the client's biography. This is especially true of psychodynamic theory, which requires the biographical information drawn from the client and focused upon by the therapist to be quite extensive. Knowledge about the immediate interactions with the environment are of secondary significance since, at best, they merely reflect patterns of behavior and response that have their origins in childhood. Anna Freud summarizes the psychodynamic focus succinctly when she writes, "Since the beginning of psychoanalysis . . . analysts have been concerned more with the era of growth and development than with maturity."[6]

The professional using a psychodynamic approach, however, tends to have little interest in happy past experiences of the client for these do not provide a basis for arriving at inferences regarding current unhappiness or troubled or troubling behavior. As Albert K. Cohen notes, psychodynamic theories appear to dwell upon the significance of—

> infantile and childhood experiences that have equipped the individual with abnormally strong or otherwise deviant or perverted needs and tendencies. For example, early unsatisfied needs for nourishment, attention, or love may leave a lifelong abiding, compulsive tendency to seize or acquire what they have been denied, or its symbolic equivalent. Or, early frustrations and harsh treatment may create enduring hostilities toward the world in general, or toward particular kinds of objects—say, maternal or parental representatives; hostilities so intense that they repeatedly break through even a strong system of controls.[7]

It is possible to note that this conviction that childhood events are said to profoundly effect one's later life is reserved for patients and clients, not ourselves. We tend to view our own adjustment and achievements as the result of our own initiatives. We are self-made; deviants are made by their parents. This form of double standard in the attribution of causation reveals the enormous amount of subjectivity permissive to practitioners who operate under this theory.

In a highly speculative and provocative book dealing with child placement and adoption, Goldstein, Freud, and Solnit utilize psychodynamic theory as a basis for their argument that adoption proceedings should not drag on interminably. The authors recommend more rapid termination of biological parents' rights in favor of those of the psychological parent, that is, caretakers who have established deep and affectionate ties with the child.[8] The thrust of their argument is that instability during childhood leads to later maladjustment. This hypothesized later maladjustment is carried forward into adulthood, thereby increasing the number of incompetent adults. They, in turn, have children, thereby weakening society.

The belief in the concept that childhood trauma is a determinant of adult deviancy is pervasive within the human service professions. At times, the application of psychodynamic theory is simplified to a direct, almost linear relationship as in the claim "abusive parents were abused themselves as children." An interesting facet of this claim is the extended dormancy period following the initial abuse that emerges years later when the victim is said to become the victimizer. Fifteen years or so go by before certain unconscious forces recreate the earlier scene with the added mind-boggling feat of role reversal. At times, the linear relationship bends to become cyclical as in the following account, "The adolescent who has a baby is trapped in a tragic cycle. Her mother probably was a teenage parent. Her baby, if it survives infancy, will likely become a teenage parent. And as an adolescent parent, this child begins a lifelong, uphill battle against poverty and divorce."[9] Anecdotal case histories or client biographies alone are cited to support these claims.

The psychodynamic perspective, which we have presented in very broad form, offers a useful approach for the human service professional. It provides a number of sensitizing concepts including the possible seriousness of childhood trauma, the role of unconscious emotions and motivations in influencing behavior, and the desirability of having the client talk about his or her problems. Where it errs and creates a potential for overreaction on the part of the human service professional is in the area of long-term prognosis. The effects of childhood trauma, as in child abuse and family separation, should be of immediate concern to the professional. When there is evidence that harm is occurring or is about to occur or that a child is endangered in the present or immediate future, the human service professional should act to protect the child. The prediction of deviancy occurring in the distant future when a child is grown, is highly speculative and supported only by retrospective studies of selected biographies that have come to the attention of human service professionals. Other cases of abuse that have entirely different outcomes, for example, where the child grows up to become a well-adjusted, successful adult, do not appear in case studies.

Eliot Freidson argues against this single-cause hypothesis in the following passage:

> [W]e are prone to assume that socialization during childhood, religious conversion, professional education, and intensive psychotherapy . . . have such permanent and significant influence on the individual that they will determine how the individual will behave in any subsequent environment . . . nonetheless we fly in the face of available evidence in believing that a critical and discrete event or process can so firmly mold the individual as to mark him for life . . . no matter what his environment.[10]

Furthermore, there is sharp disagreement among child development experts about the enduring effects of early family life on children. One group of longitudinal studies identifies the strong influence of what happens to children in their early years and its effect on their later emotional lives. Other investigators maintain that children are not quite as vulnerable as we would believe, and that people keep remaking their lives all their lives. There is no necessary connection, in the latter view, between a disadvantaged or traumatic childhood and a troubled adulthood.[11]

The theory that family life during the early years exerts a disproportionate and irreversible effect on a rapidly developing organism, compared with the potential for later environmental influences, was examined by Ann M. Clarke and A. D. B. Clarke. The authors assert that although the theory is commonly accepted by human service professionals, evidence supporting it is lacking. Despite the lack of evidence, the biographical search procedures utilized by the human service professional tend to perpetuate a continuing belief in the theory. In effect, the consequence of the choice of a single theory conditions the selectivity of the human service professional's perceptual and cognitive processes.[12] He or she searches for biographical information that fits the theory in dealing with cases and, inadvertently discards other information

that may have explanatory relevance. That is, information that is
hypothesis confirming is pursued while other information is
ignored. This process tends to both perpetuate and increase the
use of a contested theory that may have little utility in explaining
the nature of deviance. The concern with clients' biographies, the
continued use of biographical search procedures through extensive social history "taking" and other aspects in the application of
psychodynamic theory have a number of unintended effects that
may promote the continuation of deviant behavior. An exploration of the consequences of these activities will be provided in a
later chapter where the development of deviant identities will be
discussed.

MENTAL ILLNESS AND SOCIAL DEVIANCE

Human service professionals typically see individuals who are
profoundly troubled. The emotional impact of physical illness or
other disabling conditions, school failure, divorce and separation,
old age, poverty or the death of a loved one can be most distressing.
Professionals generally realize that it is the situation or event that
has led to the emotional problem the individual manifests when
they become troubled. If, however, the professionals use a psychodynamic theory to frame their perspective, their interest will be
drawn to the client's biography and the significance of the immediate contextual problem will recede somewhat. After all, the professional may note, most people at some time in their lives experience
distressing events and are able to cope with them. There must be
something about this individual that is different and prevents him
from coping successfully. A series of inferences are then made by
the professional in attempting to locate the sources of emotional
blockages or cognitive disorders in the client. Once they are located,
typically somewhere within the client's biography, they are inferred to be the cause of the current problem.

When we turn to mental illness, we find that both the theory
and the search procedure for etiology are quite different than the
process cited above. Mental illness is assumed to be the cause of
disordered behavior and the etiology is unknown and usually
unknowable. In a textbook in which the authors seek to con-

struct a theory of abnormality, Steven Reiss and others, note the dissimilarities between physical illness and mental illness:

> Diagnosis of a physical disease usually implies valid statements concerning etiology, prognosis, and treatment. For example, a diagnosis of pneumonia implies the presence of a particular bacterial infection (etiological statement), a predictable progression of the illness (prognostic statement), and the use of antibiotic drug treatment. If the classification of abnormal behaviors also permitted valid statements concerning etiology, prognosis, and treatment, it may be possible to consider the classification category a definition of a disease. However, the diagnosis of a particular kind of mental disease rarely implies any valid statements. The cause of most mental illness is unknown, the likely progression of the disorder is often unpredictable, and the appropriate treatment is only sometimes suggested by the diagnosis.[13]

Many people, including psychiatrist Thomas S. Szasz, believe the term *mental illness* is only an unproven theory used to explain behavior or unusual thought processes we do not understand and that it would be more accurate to use the term *problems in living* to explain these things.[14] There are various opinions among psychiatrists about whether or not mental illness is a disease. Further issues involve whether mental illness is a physical or psychological disease and whether it is caused by genetic defects, hormonal imbalances, or other physiological disorders or by early childhood trauma? It is sufficient to note that mental disorders are not verifiable in the same way as physical disorders.

Despite these problems we find that mental health professionals frequently claim a connection exists between mental illness and deviant behavior. That is, without knowing the cause or likely progression of mental disturbance in a patient, the mental health professional is still able to say that certain behaviors are caused by the presence of psychopathology. J. L. Simmons notes the circularity in this type of reasoning in the following quote. "People violate the norms of their group because they are psychopaths, and we know they are psychopathic because of their norm-violating behavior. Aberrant behavior is explained by internal disturbance, and internal disturbance is inferred from the aberrant behavior. 'Psychopath' is thus only a synonym for norm-violator, not an explanation."[15]

Then, it may be asked, what is the connection between mental illness and deviance? It may be correct to say that some people engage in deviant behavior because they are mentally ill. Still other people who engage in exactly the same type of deviant behavior are not mentally ill. In the early 1970s, in South America, a lone assassin attempted to kill the Pope. Despite the fact that the assassin claimed a political purpose for this act, he was declared by authorities to be mentally ill. The diagnosis provided was "systematic paranoia," a mental illness in which the individual acts normal almost all the time. By the 1980s world-wide terrorism was a recognized fact of life. So, in 1981, when another assassin shot and wounded the Pope no questions of mental illness were raised. The attempt was accepted as a political act. The dissimilarity between the two assassination attempts was the ascribed motives, not the behavior of the assailants.

Reiss and others identify irrationality as the single most important attribute of mental disorders: "A belief is irrational if it is false, if the individual is in a position to know it is false, and if the individual nevertheless thinks the belief to be true or acts as if it is true."[16] As we can see, however, irrational beliefs are held by people who are not mentally ill. But let us assume, for the moment, that there are mentally ill people and their condition causes their deviant behavior. In addition, we should also realize that there are mentally ill people, such as recluses, who may engage in bizarre or exceptional behavior that is not considered deviant.

Much reclusive behavior is, by definition, hidden from the view of others. So, if a person has no friends or visitors, rarely ventures outside his home where he lives alone and refuses to answer the doorbell, he will be seen by neighbors as strange, perhaps even antisocial, but not truly deviant, only different.

Finally, there are mentally ill people who are not now and never will be in treatment with mental health professionals. Many of these persons are located in situations where no one knows that they are mentally ill, least of all themselves. They will go through life being accommodated by their families, and their quirks and "hang-ups" will be rationalized as minor deviations or acceptable peculiarities by people around them. Estimates of rates of persons treated for mental illness compared with rates for those who are untreated are very low.[17] One investigator, summarizing the research on the issue reports that studies of specific communities suggest that when criteria for mental illness are applied to general populations, the prevalence rates for the untreated populations are several times greater than those for populations under treatment. "Thus, at least by certain criteria, there are many more people in the population who are psychologically impaired than are receiving psychiatric care at any given time."[18]

Presumably, if there was a relationship between mental illness and deviance, then untreated mentally ill populations would become known through their behavior and the gap between rates of untreated and treated persons would narrow. This has not happened. Other investigators estimate that "Nearly 90 percent of mental illness escapes recognition and, consequently, any possibility of treatment, control, or prevention."[19]

The point is that there is no necessary connection between mental illness and deviance, and no causal relationships have been established in epidemiological studies. S. Kirson Weinberg makes a useful distinction between disordered behavior (mental illness) and socially deviant behavior with reference to internal and external conflict that people may experience. He identifies disordered behavior as the result of sustained personal conflict and personality disorganization while deviant behavior is a result of social definitions and social expectations.[20]

THE PSYCHOLOGY OF DEVIANT ACTS

All acts, deviant or normative, have psychological components. The actor moves about, interacts with others, and makes his or her way in the world as a consequence of physiological and psychological needs and desires. Acts generally have motivational, cognitive, and emotional significance to the actor. Acts are also social facts since most people generally engage in behaviors that others expect of them. We greet people, stop our cars at red lights, celebrate holidays, and line up to buy tickets to plays, movies, and sports events. As we do these things, we observe norms or social expectations. Explanations for behavior can be made by reference to psychological or sociological theories or even by applying knowledge about biology, such as instinct, or physiology, which is used in explaining epilepsy. The choice of theory to explain phenomena, in this case the behavior of people, is relative to the level of explanation one wishes to achieve. As Ferdinand notes,

> Most theorists today readily admit that although their particular viewpoint is effective in explaining phenomena at a given level of analysis, phenomena at other levels must be explained by other theoretical points of view. Thus sociologists usually do not presume to suggest to the psychologists that the principles of mental behavior are implicit in the laws that govern society, and most modern psychologists realize that the principles of social organization cannot be inferred from the conscious or unconscious patterns of the human mind.[21]

One may find, however, that the theory selected fails to show unequivocally how certain behavioral patterns arise, for example, violent criminal activity. One person may engage in this type of crime through a set of circumstances and personality factors that are conducive to this type of activity. Another may engage in violent crime due to an entirely different set of circumstances and personality factors that fail to inhibit the individual from hurting other people. Still other people have been known to lead peaceful lives until they murder their spouses. There is simply too much diversity in those behaviors known as violent crime to try to explain them through a single theory or even a set of theories.

An additional requirement of a theory is that it must be specific. A theory that attempts to explain assaultive sexual behavior, robbery and "drug dealing" in the same set of terms will fail to explain why one individual engages in one of these acts while another individual engages in another. In order to rationalize this problem in theory construction it is necessary to locate something that people who commit these acts have in common that others do not.

In psychology the term *personality disorders* is intended to serve as a unifying theme that is useful in defining a diverse group of people who engage in life-long patterns of maladaptive behavior. This theme poses that there are "types of personalities" that are bent or mis-shaped (typically as a result of early childhood experiences) that cause the individuals so affected to be prone to engage in patterns of extended deviant behavior. It is said that personality disorders are distinguished from neuroses by their duration since the latter states are conceptualized as a reaction to stress occurring during a particular life period. Personality disorders are distinguished from psychoses in that they are less maladaptive and occur without accompanying hallucinations or delusions.[22]

Among the personality disorders, which include such diverse types as obsessive-compulsive personality, inadequate personality, and hysterical personality, is a disorder that has received a considerable amount of attention and relates directly to what we identify as deviant behavior. This disorder is "variously called psychopathy, sociopathy, or antisocial personality (and) because psychopaths are capable of brutal acts of aggression and ruthless acts of criminality, psychopathy has been called the most destructive and costly form of psychopathology."[23] *Psychopathic personality* is a term attributed to people who are said to lack a conscience, showing no guilt or remorse or humane regard for others as they engage in deviant behavior.

The difficulty this formulation presents for the human service professional is that it is almost entirely descriptive. Psychopaths, in addition to involvement in deviant behavior, are noted to be of average or above intelligence, at times charming, manipulative, impulsive, unreliable, insincere, egocentric, impoverished in affective relationships, uninsightful, and fail to follow any life plan.[24] Is it the salience of any one characteristic that defines psychopathy or each of them taken together? Many delinquents, alcoholics, and prostitutes are thought to be psychopathic while others are not. Is the distinction to be made on the basis of subjective judgments about the above factors?

A focus on determining etiology of psychopathy presents similar problems. In a review of the research on the causes of psychopathy in males, Reiss and others note that "these findings suggest that marital discord preceding parental separation may be a crucial factor associated with psychopathic development."[25] In a study of ten young, female prostitutes, who were said to have "borderline character pathology," two child psychiatrists generalize their findings by indicating that "the type of woman who is attracted to prostitution has had a high degree of chaos in her family background. Separation from parents, incest, child abuse, and gross neglect are common in this group."[26] One must approach etiology cautiously, however, since most people who come from broken or chaotic homes are not psychopathic. In addition, the available data on etiology of psychopathy are correlational and do not permit inferences of causality.

Psychopathic personality, is at best, a catch-all term for behavior that we don't like. In this way it most closely resembles deviance. Psychopathy is nastier than mental illness in the sense that the person knows what he or she is doing and sees nothing wrong with it. While it may be useful as a gross category to distinguish between types of disorders, its utility as an explanatory theory is highly questionable as it offers no more than synonyms in place of explanations.

THE BEHAVIORAL APPROACH

Another psychological orientation, one derived from learning theory, is the behavioral approach or behavior modification. Exponents of this school present a conception of deviance as being behavior that is learned in accordance with the same principles by which normal behavior is learned. As Leonard Ullman and Leonard Krasner note, "The behaviors traditionally called abnormal are no different quantitatively or qualitatively in their development and maintenance from other behaviors."[27] Themes presented by behavior modification include (a) conforming and deviant behavior arise from similar sources; (b) the individual cannot be considered as an entity apart from the social system in which he behaves; and (c) *abnormal, pathological,* and *deviant* are terms bestowed on individuals by society.

In part, behavior modification evolved as a reaction to the psychodynamic school that emphasized a medical approach to problems and excessive concern with the etiology of abnormal behavior. R. J. Turner and J. Cummings comment directly on these points: "The explicit attitude or mental habit of viewing behavioral deviations as symptoms of some inner pathogenic element, which must be identified through accurate diagnosis in order to know how to treat it, reflects an assumption that organic disease and psychological disorder are structurally and etiologically isomorphic. Such an assumption is neither theoretically nor experimentally defensible."[28]

Instead, behaviorists view disturbed, deviant, or difficult behavior in an individual as essentially a social phenomenon occurring as one aspect of a system, reflecting some dysfunction in that system, and best treated by some modification of that system. In the behavioral view the term "system" consists of persons in mutual interaction, such as family, school, playmates, and intimate relationships. Behaviorists often draw a distinction between the conditions that led to the original development of abnormal behavior and the conditions that currently maintain it. For example, an adolescent may begin shoplifting because of feelings of social deprivation and isolation, but continue the behavior because of the attention received when stolen goods are distributed to friends.

Since all behavior is learned, the distinction between normal and abnormal behavior is determined by society. Abnormal behavior is that which society labels as abnormal. A straightforward social definition is indicated by Ullman and Krasner who note, "Abnormality is that sort of deviance that calls for and sanctions the professional attention of psychiatrists, clinical psychologists, and other 'mental health' professionals."[29] The distinction between abnormal and normal behavior is not intrinsic to the individual: it is a judgment made by other members of society about that individual. It is not until another party observes the behavior and finds it to be problematic that it is considered to be deviant. Once the deviant is recognized and brought to the attention of a socially sanctioned labeler, that is a human service professional, he or she is given a designation, which then legitimizes the steps taken to alter the behavior.[30]

In the view of the behaviorists, then, deviant behavior cannot be defined categorically. Members of the social audience dictate the standards for deviant and acceptable behavior. It is not the presence of mental illness that determines if an individual will be hospitalized, for example, but the family's tolerance for upsetting or disturbing behavior among its members. The determination of deviance is, therefore, a subjective phenomena, influenced by the individual, the social audience, and the human service professional. A theory that accounts for the interactions of these three agents in creating deviance is necessary to fully understand what deviant behavior is. Such a theory will be presented in Chapter 4. Before we describe that theory it is necessary to explore another range of theories that have implications for the work of human service professionals. These theories are termed sociological; while they are less frequently drawn upon by human service professionals than are the psychological theories, they do tend to influence their perspectives. Since the impact of these sociological theories on professionals is more general, they will be presented in a summary or overview format.

REFERENCES

1. Albert K. Cohen, *Deviance and Control* (Engelwood Cliffs, New Jersey: Prentice-Hall, Inc., 1966) p. 41.
2. Theodore N. Ferdinand, *Typologies of Delinquency* (New York: Random House, 1966) p. 45.
3. Cohen, *Deviance and Control*, p. 45.
4. Cohen, *Deviance and Control*, p. 42.
5. Cohen, *Deviance and Control*, p. 43.
6. Anna Freud, *Normality and Pathology in Childhood* (New York: International Universities Press, 1956) p. 1.
7. Cohen, *Deviance and Control*, p. 55.
8. Joseph Goldstein, Anna Freud, and Albert J. Solnit, *Beyond the Best Interests of the Child* (New York: The Free Press, 1973) pp. 32, 35.
9. *Detroit Free Press*, Nov. 8, 1981, p. 13.
10. Eliot Freidson, *Professional Dominance: The Social Structure of Medical Care* (Chicago: Aldine Publishing Company, 1970) pp. 56–66.
11. Albert Rosenfeld, "The 'Elastic Mind' Movement: Rationalizing Child Neglect?", *Saturday Review, 4:* 1, 1978.
12. Ann M. Clarke and A. D. B. Clarke, *Early Experience: Myth and Evidence* (London: Open Books, 1975).
13. Steven Reiss and others, *Abnormality: Experimental and Clinical Approaches* (New York: Macmillan Publishing Co., Inc., 1977) pp. 59–60.
14. Thomas S. Szasz, *Ideology and Insanity* (Garden City, New York: Doubleday & Company, Inc., 1970.) p. 13.
15. Jerry L. Simmons, *Deviants* (The Glendassary Press, 1969) p. 14.
16. Reiss and others, *Abnormality*, p. 65.
17. B. Pasamanick, "A Survey of Mental Disease in an Urban Population, IV. An Approach to Total Prevalence Rates," *Archives of General Psychiatry, 5:* 151–155, 1971; and L. Strole and others, *Mental Health in the Metropolis* (New York: McGraw-Hill, 1962).

18. Howard B. Kaplan, "Mental Illness as a Social Problem," in *Handbook on the Study of Social Problems*, ed. Erwin O. Smigel (Chicago: Rand McNally and Company, 1971) p. 332.
19. R. J. Plunkett and J. E. Gordon, *Epidemiology and Mental Illness* (New York: Basic Books, 1960) p. 5.
20. S. Kirson Weinberg, "Disordered Behavior," in *Sociology of Mental Disorders*, ed. S. Kirson Weinberg (Chicago: Aldine Publishing Company, 1967) p. 166.
21. Ferdinand, *Typologies of Delinquency*, pp. 20–21.
22. Reiss and others, *Abnormality*, pp. 368–69.
23. Reiss and others, *Abnormality*, p. 371.
24. H. Cleckley, *The Mask of Sanity*, 5th ed. (St. Louis: The C. V. Mosby Co., 1976), p. 178.
25. Reiss and others, *Abnormality*, p. 874.
26. Katherine MacVicar and Marcia Dillon, "Childhood and Adolescent Development of Ten Female Prostitutes." *Journal of Child Psychiatry, 19,* (1) (Winter): 146, 1980.
27. Leonard Ullman and Leonard Krasner, *A Psychological Approach to Abnormal Behavior* (Englewood Cliffs, N.J.: Prentice-Hall, 1969) p. 5.
28. R. J. Turner and J. Cumming, "Theoretical Malaise and Community Mental Health," in *Emergent Approaches to Health Problems*, eds. E. L. Cowen, E. A. Gardiner, and M. Zax (New York: Appleton–Century Crofts, 1967) pp. 40–62.
29. Ulman and Krasner, *A Psychological Approach*, p. 7.
30. Leonard Ullman, "Behavior Therapy as Social Movement," in *Behavior Therapy: Appraisal and Status*, ed. Cyril Franks (New York: McGraw-Hill Book Company, 1969) p. 498.

Chapter 3

ETIOLOGIES OF DEVIANCE

Sociological Views

Sociology, like psychology, is the study of human behavior. While there is no universally agreed upon definition of sociology, Arnold M. Rose offers one that is probably acceptable to most sociologists, "Sociology is the science of interaction among people and the effects of this interaction on human behavior."[1] Unlike psychology, however, sociology shows little concern for the family biographies of individuals and instead focuses on systems or structures that impact on people, for example, laws, cultures, neighborhoods, and organizations, that are said to account for differences among people.

Sociologists regard personality as mostly the product of internalized cultures that are lodged within the social structure of a particular society. It is assumed in sociological inquiry that some features of social structure and culture are critically important and enduring and they provide limits or provocations within which particular social situations can occur. As the sociologist Albert Cohen notes, "Different kinds of deviant acts are variously distributed within a given social structure, and these distributions differ from one time to another and from one structure to another."[2]

Prostitution, then, is relative to the roles of women in a society, how they are socialized into these roles and the social forces and cultural conditions that maintain them in these roles, which, on occasion, fail. Similarly, alcoholism can be viewed as a by-product of a society's culture, its customs related to drinking such as celebrations, as well as public policies regarding the advertising, distribution, sale and availability of alcoholic beverages.

The sociologists' interest in the subject of murder may lead to an examination of the differential in rates of homicide between

42

men and women, or young men versus older men, or its incidence
in urban versus suburban areas, or a comparison of its frequency
during different historical periods. Psychologists, on the other
hand, tend to be interested in the attributes or characteristics of
the murderer, his motivation or perhaps his biography.

Those sociological theories that most closely relate to problems
of social deviance have been termed social pathology, social disorganization and anomie theory. These theories are concerned with
the discovery of those elements in the social structure that produce rates and patterns of deviance in a society. That is, etiologies
of deviant behavior are said to exist somewhere in the fabric of
society and subsequently affect the psychology of the individual
actor. The treatment of the three theories that follows is not meant
to be a full exposition but it is intended as a commentary on each
relevant to the understanding and work world of the human service professional.

SOCIAL PATHOLOGY

Social pathology is an old term, derived from European theorists
of the nineteenth century and applied to identified social problems in the United States around the beginning of the twentieth
century. In the United States, it marked the fusing of sociology
and social casework around a rudimentary medical perspective.
As Goode observes, "Its central assumptions are that society is
very much like an organism and deviance is very much like a
disease. . . . Deviance is harmful, it arises from pathological conditions, and it is intrinsically unnatural."[3]

Pathology referred to abnormalities in the social system, the
presence of inferior populations, delinquents, and dependent
classes who had failed to adjust to a near perfect society. In
Nanette Davis' view the central concern of the social pathologists was fixed on certain populations: "The notion of adjustment implies, on the one hand, that there is an ordered society
of competent, middle-class, success-oriented persons, and, on the
other, that there are misfits who fail to adapt to institutional
requirements and goals. What reformers, social workers, and
pathologists had in mind was the immigrant, who manifested

symptoms of 'social breakdown, disturbance, and dislocation.' "[4]

The social pathologists likened society to a human organism, which can suffer ill-health and be cured, and therefore the medical implications of their language were used metaphorically rather than analogously. Implicit in this view of social pathology are sets of assumptions about what society should be like and what normal human behavior is. The early social pathologist view was biased from a middle-class value preference and preoccupied with corrective remedies for individual problems. As Davis observes, "The model of social organizations . . . adapted was that of a small town blown up in scale. The good society was one in which the intimacy and homogeneity of primary groups prevailed, social change occurred in a gradual and orderly fashion, and citizens were adjusted, neighborly, and helpful."[5]

Later social pathologists, recognizing the inevitability of urbanization and industrialization, began to focus on these and associated factors as contributing to such social problems as delinquency, alcoholism, and prostitution. Their view was one of the essential goodness of people who are negatively affected by deleterious social conditions and deviance as one product of these conditions. The early social pathologists saw the need to correct values as the pathway to remediation. The values of immigrants and other city dwellers were not adaptive to the complexities and difficulties of urban life. Later social pathologists drew attention to the conditions as being in need of change. Both views were essentially value orientations, that is, they were not arrived at empirically; therefore, they have been rejected by mainstream sociology.

Social work, however, drew its positive view of humanity from this source and not the perspectives embedded in psychodynamic theory of innate or instinctual drives, untamed libidinal strivings, and fixations derived from frustrated childhood. While the so-called underclass was infected by "social pathology," remediation was not only possible but highly desirable. People can not only change for the better but will inevitably do so when they live under positive social conditions. Social pathologists viewed the individual as malleable, given the proper life circumstances and living conditions. Goals expressed by social pathologists include reform of social institutions and to increase governmental expenditures for programs to improve housing and employment opportunities and to reduce discrimination.

Such goals are nonsensical when one takes a psychodynamic approach since their realization cannot change the "kinds of people" whose behavioral patterns are truly obnoxious and determined many years earlier. How would one convince the social worker and psychiatrist who wrote the following statement:

> Many of the parents of juvenile delinquents who are seen (here) . . . may be said to have character disorders. They have primitive ego structures, and their defenses and ways of gratifying themselves are clearly related to pregenital (oral or anal) levels of psychosexual development. It is our belief that it is the clients who fall within this group who have caused social workers to regard parents of delinquents as difficult or impossible to treat. Persons with this same syndrome also become clients of relief agencies, medical clinics, child placing agencies, and so on, where they present similar problems. They are full of resistance; they break appointments; they withhold information; they becloud issues in a variety of ways. They relate to other people in a primitive and often distorted fashion. . . . [6]

While this is not a very encouraging or optimistic statement the article does go on to indicate that years of casework treatment may bring about some change in "character structure."[7]

Actually, the above quote does have a direct relationship to the social pathologists who gained preeminence around the beginning of the twentieth century. They opened doors for a dual approach within social work. Since pathology was rampant in the cities, restoration of the urban area was one approach. Another was to view the impoverished city dweller as a patient and the family as diseased. These were maladjusted persons who needed remediation or treatment. Youth who became delinquent needed to have their environments changed and be provided with the proper socialization they had never received. People were not seen as competent to make suitable decisions and judgements; these had to be done for them. Extended treatment was required to bring about change since the process of urban debasement had gone on for so many years.

SOCIAL DISORGANIZATION

The social disorganization school of sociology followed the social pathologists and focused on the effects of urbanization as it impacted on individuals. They saw that impersonal relations between people prevailed; primary ties had broken down as a result of diversity and competition. As Davis notes,

> "this new historical reality presented an anomaly. On the one hand, close physical proximity connected persons and groups who shared few similarities in tastes, habits, or language. Slum dwellers and gold coast residents were geographical neighbors. On the other hand, cultural, economic, and political barriers divided classes, occupations, group. Social relations were typically competitive, often antagonistic."[8]

Old norms and behavior patterns were obsolete and insufficient, incapable of helping the individual cope with new life-styles in the city. Family relations and norms, particularly authority relationships, were disrupted because they failed to fit the new social environment.

What is this new social environment and why does it present these difficulties? Social disorganization theorists suggested one should look to the old to understand the problem. As Robert E. Park notes, "Until a few years ago the typical American was . . . an inhabitant of a middle western village; such a village, perhaps, as Sinclair Lewis described in *Main Street*."[9] The new and problematic social environment consists of "great cities, with the vast division of labor which has come in with machine industry, and with movement and change that have come about with the multiplication of the means of transportation and communication, [consequently] the old forms of social control represented by the family, the neighborhood, and the local community have been undermined and their influence greatly diminished."[10] The emphasis, within the social disorganization school, is placed on the effects of pressures that originate outside a given system, such as the family or peer group associations, and that require adaptations within the system to cope adequately with a changed environment. In essence, the cause of disorganization is seen as resulting from external forces impinging on intact but nonadaptive social systems.[11]

The connection between the theory of social disorganization and social deviance was bridged by a group of sociologists who were interested in the ecology of the city. More specifically, they were concerned with the effects of social change on social order in urban areas. They operated on the assumption that rates for deviant behavior can serve as evidence of social disorganization. As Robert E. L. Faris and H. Warren Dunham, two leading ecologists observe, "A relationship between urbanism and social disorganization has long been recognized and demonstrated. Crude rural–urban comparisons of rates of dependency, crime, divorce and desertion, suicide, and vice have shown these problems to be more severe in the cities, especially the large rapidly expanding industrial cities."[12] A circular perspective developed wherein it was maintained that a set of processes or patterns labeled as social disorganization could also be used to explain certain undesirable forms of behavior. In other words, "Those societies which exhibit a high degree of social disorganization will also be found to contain much crime, alcoholism, and mental disorder."[13] An external force such as economic depression, in this view, creates unemployment, which, in turn, alters family roles, leading to conflict and demoralization, contributing to individual maladaptations such as mental illness, suicide, and crime.

The contribution of social disorganization theory to the human service professional is a perspective that claims that much deviant behavior on the part of individuals is not pathological but rather a consequence of social and environmental conditions. For example, Faris and Dunham report that many types of deviance, including mental disorders, are more prevalent in highly disorganized areas of the city than in more organized ones. Various efforts of reform were initiated by human service workers at the time including prevention programs of various types, public education for adults, and a considerable amount of "grass roots" organizing, all legacies that continue today.

In addition, ethnographies or case studies of natural systems such as street corner life were provided that examined deviant groups in detail, portraying complex and highly organized sets of relationships. Street gang life was seen as richly organized, hierarchical, and a means for preserving, not destroying values.[15]

Delinquency was transmitted through such groups as a normal, naturally occurring event.[16] Deviant types were made, not born, through social processes that occurred in isolated settings apart from the mainstream of society. These ethnographies served to bridge the theoretical gap between social breakdown, for example broken homes, poverty, and urban slums, and social deviance with which they were correlated.

ANOMIE THEORY

Anomie is a general term that has been used by Emile Durkheim to signify that during periods of sudden social change the norms that traditionally regulate people break down. Durkheim notes, for example, that "When society is disturbed by some painful crisis or by beneficient but abrupt transitions, it is momentarily incapable of exercising this (normative) influence; thence come the sudden rises in the curve of suicides."[17] It is social change that creates unfamiliar situations for people that leads to an increase in indicators of pathology, including suicide, which had historically been regarded as highly individualistic phenomena.

Robert K. Merton, in further developing anomie theory, proposed a perspective that specifically focused on an explanation for deviance when he wrote. "Some unknown but substantial proportion of deviant behavior does not represent impulses of individual breaking through social control, but, on the contrary, represents socially induced deviations which the culture and the social organization conjoin to produce."[18]

Merton's general theory of deviant behavior proposed that first, there are culture goals that are sought after goods and services that people are taught to want by their culture. Second, there are the norms prescribing the means that may be legitimately employed in the pursuit of these goals. Third, there are institutionalized means or "the actual distribution of facilities and opportunities for achieving the culture goals in a manner compatible with the norms."[19]

All people in American society are influenced by the culture goals, both for their intrinsic value and their symbolic worth. They consist of objects that can be enjoyed and consumed and provide additional satisfactions by gaining the emulation of others for their owners. Success goals are disseminated during childhood socialization, continually emphasized by the mass media, and made apparent on a daily basis through the differential handling of poor people in public schools, playgrounds, and clinics. For a considerable part of the same population, however, the social structure restricts or closes off access to approved modes of reaching these goals creating strain toward deviant behavior ensuing on a large scale.[20] That is, given the internalization of achievement norms and the structural blockages impeding legitimate solutions by individuals, some are likely to pursue illegitimate solutions. The requisite conditions for anomie are present when members of some segments of society such as the poor or certain racial-ethnic minorities are constantly informed through the media and popular myth that monetary success and its material rewards are goals that are positively valued, while at the same time their experience tells them that the legitimate means for achieving these goals are relatively unavailable to them.[21] The manual worker, trapped in a no-win, low-esteem job, "infected with the contagion of success goals," but denied a means for achieving them, withdraws through drugs, alcohol, or mental illness or struggles ahead through criminal enterprise.[22] The attentuation between goals and means causes anomie or a state of normlessness among sectors of the population. Merton identifies the one positive adaptation to the situation as *innovation,* and labels three other deviant adaptations as *ritualism, retreatism,* and *rebellion.*

Richard A. Cloward has further developed anomie theory with special attention to juvenile delinquency. His formulation poses that just as there are differentials in regard to legitimate opportunity structures there are variations in access to illegitimate means. Lower class people, for example, do not have access to white collar criminal roles, and most would not have the opportunity to join established criminal syndicates. Cloward also views retreatist adaptations as occurring not only as a response to failure in conventional society but also arising "with considerable frequency among those who are failures in both worlds, conventional and illegitimate alike."[23] Cloward, collaborating with Lloyd E. Ohlin elaborated on these themes to explain gang or subcultural delinquency that develops when success goals are internalized but are prevented from being realized due to limited educational and economic means.[24]

Strains in the social structure, including poverty amidst a consumption-oriented society; restricted opportunities for some and enhanced options for others; and discrimination against the lower class and advantage to the upper class, create personal stress leading some people and groups to resort to deviant adaptations.

Anomie theory does not account for all forms of deviant behavior nor does it specify the precise conditions that join to promote deviant behavior by some persons and not others. Sexual deviations such as incest and rape, drug use by successful individuals, and certain other forms of deviance do not seem to fit within this formulation. Anomie theory is best applied to lower class delinquent and criminal behavior, but it does present implications that are applicable to conditions faced by the lower class in general that interface with the work of human service professionals.

If deviance is an outcome of actual and perceived deprivation, then programs that increase opportunities for lower class persons and ethnic minorities are necessary. Such programs would involve skill training of lower-class adolescents that would prepare them for a step beyond the bottom rung of the labor market ladder, improved educational opportunities, the creation of jobs with potential for advancement, and enhanced options for better housing and living conditions. Anomie theory does not imply that these social benefits be distributed to all; only that the opportunity to compete for them be available to all.

SOME THOUGHTS ON THEORIES

The claim that deviants are psychologically abnormal persons is false. Some are; many are not. In part, this claim arose from investigators applying a specific psychological theory to cases that were being seen in clinical practice. Such cases are selective in that they were persons who, perhaps, sought therapy, as a consequence of feeling guilty about their participation in deviant behavior. Other investigators saw referred cases, that is, deviants pressured into seeking therapy as an alternative to sentencing by courts.

These are deviants who have "failed" in the sense that they were caught by the authorities or their own consciences. We doubt that successful deviants such as crime syndicate bosses, international drug smugglers, and leaders of revolutionary groups can be considered psychologically abnormal persons. As Gibbons and Jones note, "Our judgment is that there probably are many deviants who are psychologically well adjusted and who exhibit quite conventional personality configurations."[25]

The sociological perspective of the social disorganization and anomie schools contend that during periods of social strain large numbers of normal but poor people, facing added stress, will be pushed into deviance. A concern with rates of deviance fails to focus on the psychological processes involved in the manufacture of deviance and why two persons facing similar degrees of stress select or yield to different adaptations. But, sociological theory does inform us that psychological interpretations alone are insufficient since they have not incorporated the sources of strain existing in society that lead to patterns of deviant behavior.

While both psychological and sociological theories attempt to account for the same behavior, deviance, the levels of explanation are sharply divergent. The former set of theories explore emotions, motivations, and the way people learn. The latter group of theories utilize and explore variables on a much more abstract level, such as changing social and economic conditions, social–structural strain, and opportunity structures that impact on people. What is lacking in both groups of theories is an interactional theme, one that offers an explanation of the particular interactions between the individual and society that leads to deviance. As Goode observes, interactionist theories have built into their analysis of deviance "an active, self-aware, and voluntaristic subject," who is not a passive "receptacle of overwhelming forces from within or without," but "possesses a will."[26] On the other hand, "non-interactionist theories match up an initial pre-existing condition with a certain type of outcome—commiting a deviant act."[27]

REFERENCES

1. Arnold M. Rose, *Sociology,* Second ed. (New York: Alfred Knopf, Publishers, 1965) p. 3.
2. Albert K. Cohen, *Deviance and Control* (Englewood Cliffs, New Jersey: Prentice-Hall, Inc., 1966) pp. 45–46.
3. Erich Goode, *Deviant Behavior: An Interactionist Approach* (Englewood Cliffs, New Jersey: Prentice-Hall, Inc., 1978) pp. 21–22
4. Nanette J. Davis, *Sociological Constructions of Deviance: Perspectives and Issues in the Field* (Dubuque, Iowa: Wm. C. Brown Company Publishers, 1975) p. 27.
5. Davis, *Sociological Constructions,* p. 33.
6. Beatrice R. Simcox and Irving Kaufman, "Treatment of Character Disorders in Parents of Delinquents," *Social Casework,* Oct./ Nov.: 3–18, 1956.
7. Simcox and Kaufman, "Character Disorders in Parents," 3.
8. Davis, *Sociological Constructions,* pp. 39–40.
9. Robert E. Park, "Social Change and Social Disorganization," in *The City,* eds. Robert E. Park, Ernest W. Burgess, and Roderick D. McKenzie (Chicago: The University of Chicago, 1967) p. 105.
10. Robert E. Park, "Social Change" p. 106.
11. Arnold M. Rose, "History and Sociology of the Study of Social Problems." in *Handbook on the Study of Social Problems,* ed. Erwin O. Smigel (Chicago: Rand McNally and Company, 1971) p. 25.
12. Robert E. L. Faris and H. Warren Dunham, *Mental Disorders in Urban Areas* (Chicago: The University of Chicago, 1967) p. 1.
13. Don C. Gibbons and John F. Jones, *The Study of Deviance: Perspectives & Problems* (Englewood Cliffs, New Jersey: Prentice-Hall, 1975) p. 18.
14. Faris and Dunham, *Mental Disorders,* p. 21.
15. William F. Whyte, *Street Corner Society: The Social Structure of an Italian Slum* (Chicago: University of Chicago Press, 1943).
16. Clifford R. Shaw and Henry D. McKay, "Male Juvenile Delinquency as Group Behavior," in *The Social Fabric of the Metropolis,* ed. J. F. Short, Jr. (Chicago: University of Chicago Press, 1971).
17. Emile Durkheim, *Suicide,* trans. J. A. Spaulding and G. Simpson (New York: The Free Press, 1951), p. 252.
18. Robert K. Merton, "The Social-Cultural Environment and Anomie," in *New Perspectives for Research on Juvenile Delinquency,* eds. Helen L. Witmer and Ruth Kotinsky (Washington, D.C.), p. 83.
19. Cohen, *Deviance and Control,* p. 76.
20. Merton, *Social Theory,* p. 146.
21. Stuart H. Traub and Craig B. Little, eds., *Theories of Deviance* (2nd Ed.) Itasca, Illinois: F. E. Peacock Publishers, Inc., 1980) p. 94.
22. Davis, *Sociological Construction,* p. 102.
23. Richard A. Cloward, "Illegitimate Means, Anomie, and Deviant Behavior," *American Sociological Review, 24* (April): 164–176, 1959.

24. Richard A. Cloward and Lloyd E. Ohlin, *Delinquency and Opportunity: A Theory of Delinquent Gangs* (New York: The Free Press of Glencoe, 1960).
25. Gibbons and Jones, *Study of Deviance,* p. 121.
26. Goode, *Deviant Behavior,* p. 175.
27. Goode, *Deviant Behavior,* p. 116.

Chapter 4

AN INTERACTIONIST THEORY OF DEVIANCE

THE INTERACTIONIST PERSPECTIVE

When people arrive at impressions of others, they are engaging in typing or typification. The impression that is gained is in part based upon immediate observation and in part based on images dredged up from past encounters or things that we have heard about or read about. How people typify one another and how they relate to one another based on these judgements is the central concern of the interactionist perspective.

One interactionist perspective that has been proposed to study and explain deviance consists of a three-step interaction process. The process begins with the original behavior and then moves on to the negative social reaction to that behavior. The final step in the process is the response or adjustment of the individual to that reaction. A key element in step two, which serves to organize and unify the social reaction, is the designation of a label to fit the individual who exhibited the original behavior. "Labeling theory" is the name given to the set of concepts to be examined in this chapter.

A case illustration at this point may be useful to identify how the concepts of typing and labeling occur in the actual experiences of people:

> He knew he wasn't stupid but Mike, eleven years old, somehow could not comprehend what he was reading. Mike is a pupil who suffers from an unknown and undiagnosed learning disability. He sits in the classroom alongside his peers but is unable to comprehend both the written and verbal work expected of him. He cannot follow the reading material or transfer written material to his notebook or grasp the concepts presented by the teacher within the alloted time periods. As a result he feels frustrated and isolated.
>
> Mike's teacher is not quite sure what to make of him. She tries a number

of different approaches but finally becomes frustrated herself. Subsequently, Mike is alternately ignored, cajoled and then ridiculed before the other pupils. Eventually they begin to focus on his inadequacies and he is taunted and mimicked in the classroom and on the playground.

It is evident that the first two steps in the interaction process have occurred. Mike's difficulty in learning, in keeping up with his fellow students, is the original behavior. The negative social reaction to that behavior is expressed first by the teacher and subsequently by Mike's peers. An additional reaction is then achieved through the teacher's contact with Mike's parents. As a result of this contact Mike's parents attempt to force him to spend more time working at home on his studies. They cut off his television viewing, weekend attendance at movies, and the like. Continuing failure at school and negative reports from the teacher lead the parents to enact even harsher punishments and deprivations at home.

What is Mike to do? The social reaction to Mike's school behavior is uniformly negative and extends into his home and leisure time. He can assume the role of class "dummy," accept the view of others about himself and hope that by becoming ingratiating the punishments will be modified. Or, as is the case, he begins to associate with other pupils who are known to be not only disaffected by school but are seen as being bad, tough, troublemakers. Mike begins to develop quite a different reputation; as a truant, bully, and fighter. The degree of acceptance by his new friends increases. These friendships become even more important to Mike as this occurs, and his attitude change intensifies. The new role, while not being one that Mike originally chose for himself, is eminently more satisfying to him than that of class "dummy." Mike's adjustment to the reaction of others to his original behavior is complete.

A psychological analysis of Mike's case would lead one to the conclusion that the cause of the problem was a learning disability. However, this could only be considered to be an original cause and not the effective cause. While it is true that if Mike didn't have a learning disability the negative sequence would not have occurred, it is equally true that the learning disability did not cause the teacher, the other pupils and Mike's parents to react in the ways they did. In addition, the social reaction did not force Mike to become a rebel. At play are some very complex processes which need to be examined in order to gain an understanding of these phenomena. The terms used to explore these processes include *labels* and *labeling, primary* and *secondary deviance,* and *stereotyping.* The focus of concern is with those people known as deviants.

> Who are the deviants? They are by no means a homogeneous group, and the symptoms that mark them for societal attention are not simple to classify. The earmarks of some are predominantly medical — the schizophrenic, the manic-depressive, the senile. Others may manifest their deviance through intellectual, chronological, social, economic, sexual, or doctrinal nonconformity. . . . Contemporary Americans may have a reasonably broad consensus regarding some of those labeled deviant such as the violent sex offender or the . . . disturbed juvenile delinquent. Social agreement may be increasingly tenuous regarding many others who are labeled deviants for less hazardous social behavior such as the truant child, the excessive drinker, or the promiscuous welfare recipient.
>
> Some deviants, while socially maladjusted or psychologically abnormal, are comparatively innocuous: the senile old lady who nightly roams the streets; . . . the school dropout; the vagrant; or the teenage girl who runs away from home. Others, however, are a major menace to society. They include the habitual molester of children, the narcotics pusher, or the psychopathic mass-killer.[2]

The deviants identified here all share one important distinction that sets them apart from others; we have names or labels for each of them. What do we mean by the term *label,* and what do labels mean to us?

A TYPOLOGY OF LABELS

The ascription of labels is a means of describing and understanding objects and events in the natural world according to some easily understood classifications. Labels are used to not only identify classes of things like fuel and furniture but also to differentiate between them, such as garbage and food, so that people do not have to examine minutely every object with which they come in contact.

People are also designated and differentiated by labels. During an earlier period persons who were ascribed the label *serf* or *slave* were bound for their lifetimes by obligations relative to their positions. Through no actions of their own these responsibilities were passed along to their children. Sometime later people were labeled by the work that they did, and names such as *Mason* and *Smith* were applied. Others received appelations from places or points of family origin, such as *field, burger,* and *towne.*

In modern times things are not nearly so clear. A diffuse and fluid social structure creates conditions in which people acquire numerous labels. People may be labeled according to, among others, gender, age, marital state, occupation, social class, amount of education, and the political party for which they vote. They are labeled by others; in turn label others; and even engage in self-labeling. Some labels, however, are more meaningful than others, and such designations can have important consequences for the bearer. It is one thing to label oneself a liberal or to be seen as one by others in a conservative community. It is quite another to be labeled psychotic and removed to a mental hospital. The consequences of the former label may be mildly negative while the latter one may result in almost total exclusion from the community.

The typology that follows is not intended as a comprehensive examination of labels but instead is presented to highlight the kinds and types that are applied to people by both general audiences and human service professionals. Our concern, ultimately, is with the effect on the bearer of the label. There are at least five ways to look at labels:

1. *Descriptive labels:* Probably the most common kind of label, these refer typically to physical characteristics that are salient in the eyes of the viewer. Other persons or oneself are described as tall, short, old, young, good looking, ugly, or even nondescript. Descriptive labels are, for the most part, representative of the perspective of the audience.

2. *Behavioral labels:* These too are popular and used commonly to refer to an observed constellation of behaviors that are shortened to a word or phrase; he is pleasant, aggressive, ignorant, smart. Like all labels, behavioral labels are "shortcuts" in communication, whereby word symbols reduce the need for further elaboration.

3. *Status labels:* There are two types of status labels: the achieved and the ascribed. Achieved status refers to occupations and posi-

tions in organizations such as banker or truck driver, teacher or airline pilot. The person is said to have gained a particular status through his or her own efforts. Ascribed status refers to gender, age, and ethnicity as in, "she is a young, black woman." The latter status designations are said to be arrived at through birth. As we shall see, the distinction between the two types of status labels is not nearly as clear as it seems. Deviant status are usually thought of as being achieved while in actuality they are largely ascribed.

4. Informal and formal labels: Informal labeling arises out of the need of people to have a fairly good idea of who others are around them and what they will do. It is the culmination of an assessment based upon cues we receive. Each of us is labeled in many ways by people with whom we come in contact. The neighbor's child may be seen as "wild" and destructive, causing the parents of other children to admonish them to avoid him. A fellow employee may be seen as temperamental and argumentative, or as a heavy drinker, or as lazy and egotistical, leading others to distrust him. The consequences of informal labels may be dire but are rarely predictably so, one may choose to ignore them.

Formal or official labels are designations arrived at through organizational processes of one kind or another. Persons are labeled by schools, courts, mental hospitals, and welfare agencies and receive such designations as retarded, criminal, mentally ill, destitute, and dependent, among others. Formal labels tend to be more potent than informal labels since they are dispensed by organizations that claim the expertise and the right to proffer these designations by society. Second, labels designated by organizations are "official" since they are usually empowered by law to engage in labeling. The effect that results is that the bearer willingly or unwillingly must carry the label; it tends to "stick" while informal labels may disappear over time. In addition, formal labels, unlike informal labels, are invariably recorded in official documents, lists, police records, insurance reports, and case records.

5. Positive and negative labels: Each of the four types of labels identified may be positive, neutral, or negative. As general types they fail to present invidious distinctions. To say "she's a married woman" means very little unless we know the context and the intention of the participants in the verbal interaction.

Examining the contextual aspect of labeling is crucial to understanding the exact nature of the label. Children can be called intelligent or dull by their school teachers, friends, or families, and the same label in each context can have entirely different meanings and ramifications. To refer to someone as sick may be an accurate description of a state of poor health or pejorative name-calling in which the person is being referred to as mentally ill.

The words *positive* and *negative* connected to some labels refer to the affect labels connote. Saying someone is tall, a descriptive label, presents no specific affect. Referring to someone as a crook generally implies negative affect. Many labels contain built-in images that convey affect to most, if not all, audiences. The announcement of Nobel Prize awards elicits positive affect while a jury verdict of guilty following a criminal trial delivers a clearly negative label.

As noted in Chapter 1 labels used to designate deviants are either intended to be negative or result in negative affect and responses by social audiences. In either case, they are always negative.

CREATING LABELS: THE SOCIAL CONSTRUCTION OF REALITY

At some point in the natural order of events people are born, eat, move from place to place, fornicate, die, get wet in the rain, dry out in the sun, and, from time to time, stumble over rocks. They are subject to natural events to which they add meaning. The phrase "social construction of reality" is provided to identify how people invent their own culture to give meaning to life.[3] The reality of natural events is given meaningful order by man. In this view, even nature, for example a very warm day, is not an "event" unless it is somehow coded into a culture that imputes significance to changes in the weather. These meanings that people add to natural events represent the creation of cultural products.

The application of labels to objects, people, and human behavior is a way of ordering things that are relevant and ultimately leads to devising cultures, with systems of rules and regulations, which are constructed out of the same need to add order and meaning to life.

Reality is continually being constructed. Innovation and invention are the terms that we use to portray positive constructions. However, the ordered reality, once constructed, is threatened by disorder and deviations from that which is seen as being desirable. These threats, for the most part, are seen as evil. Persons who engage in behavior or possess attributes that are seen as threatening become deviants.

In the United States, we are seeing a vast proliferation of official labeling. An array of labels has been constructed to account for just about all norm violations. Deviations that may have been ignored in the past are now provided with names or labels, which validates the existence of a new disorder and therefore an emerging class of deviants. Informal labels that are little more than stereotypes become formal labels. Nonconformists are subjected to organizational processing and the creation of new groups of deviants. For example, while hundreds of thousands of juveniles left home during the Great Depression in the 1930s, it was not until the 1970s that attention was drawn to "runaway youth" who were said to represent a new social problem requiring the attention of juvenile courts and other agencies.

Similarly, since the end of World War II, considerable attention has been directed toward school children who present learning difficulties as opposed to upgrading the education of children generally. This focus has introduced into the public schools a substructure of special offices, classrooms, and personnel and a very detailed, intricate series of new labels. Still, a third example of the social construction of labels is the increased concern about child abuse, a label that didn't exist forty years ago. However, the social construction of child abuse draws attention to the mistreatment of children in only one context, that of the family. It is actually family-centered child abuse about which we are concerned, not the mistreatment of children in many public schools, institutions, and congregate residential facilities.

In these ways and many others the invention and designation of labels refocuses reality by bringing certain natural or social events to the forefront of our attention, imputing negative value or disorder to them, and ultimately identifying cases that fit the label. However, the processes at work in the creation of labels are exceedingly complex, not well understood, and highly variable. At least four forces that act to create labels can be identified and examined: (1) the need for order requires explanations for disorder; (2) groups who have the power to create labels; (3) the media that promulgate labels; and (4) organizations that are responsible for handling deviations.

1. The Need for Order Requires Explanations for Disorder

An orderly world must offer explanations for disorderly events. As we add meaning to those things that matter to us (family life, safe neighborhoods, athletic events, and abundant food for example), we construct our own reality. These things are important to us not only for the gratification they bring but also because they are invested with moral value.

> Once larger numbers of the members of a society begin questioning the validity and the legitimacy of the social order and its rules, their foundation and their grip on people becomes shaky. . . . However, it is often the case that a majority believes in the validity of one set of rules. And those who believe otherwise, or who do things to contradict these rules, will be regarded with suspicion. These people are often seen as troublemakers who threaten the social order. They seem to offer an alternative way of looking at reality, at the world, at the rules. They are engaged (or some so think) in an active denial of the social order.[4]

Designations of deviance, i.e. labels, are socially constructed realities that are central to our interpretation of the world. "The social world is thus both interpreted and constructed through the medium of language. Language and language categories provide the ordered meanings by which we experience ourselves and our lives in society. They make the social world (objects, behavior, etc.) meaningful."[5] The language of deviance designations, for example, juvenile delinquent, mental illness, is acquired "as cohesive wholes and without reconstructing the original process of formation."[6] Labels, especially medical labels, in and of themselves are very often accepted as a sufficient explanation for deviant behavior.

A number of years ago a young man, carrying an assortment of rifles, climbed to the roof of a tall tower on a university campus and proceeded to shoot twenty-one people from that vantage point.

A few hours later an assault was mounted, and he was killed. The search for etiology that typically follows such events proved fruitless for he had not "been in trouble with the law," had no prior record of mental illness, came from a "good home," and had not been acting strangely prior to the shootings. No explanation for the act could be offered. Finally, a postmortem was performed, and it was discovered that he had a previously undiagnosed brain tumor. This discovery was offered as the reason for his behavior. There was no necessity to offer an explanation of the connection between the motivation to perform the act, the careful planning it involved, the physical sequence of activities necessary to carry it out, and the presence of a tumor. Somehow, the tumor was responsible, and therefore order has been returned to the universe.

This human need, the need to have our version of the world secure is buttressed by applying labels to conduct that appears to threaten it. Labels offer an explanation and simultaneously evoke a conditioned reaction in us that allows us to discount or attack the label bearer, while our version of the world remains intact. Each of us, however, does not invent a dictionary of labels to define the threats around us. That is done for us by others.

2. Groups Who Have the Power to Create Labels

The key to creation of labels is definition. How do we know that certain behaviors are deviant and not desirable? There are groups that have preceded us, and they either have the legitimacy to define deviance or are active in seeking it. For hundreds, perhaps thousands of years, ecclesiastical groups determined which behaviors were good and which were evil. More recently, groups such as the American Legion and the Moral Majority attempt to define patriotism and its opposite, treason, and subsume under the deviance of treason those acts they find to be unpatriotic.

As Howard Becker notes, deviance is always a product of enterprise, and campaigns for deviance designation are the work of "moral entrepreneurs."[7] The title Becker has introduced has been expanded to include not only those who hope to gain power by espousing their version of morality but also others who seek to advance themselves and their organizations, causes, and professions. Contemporary antiabortion and antipornography groups are examples of the original meaning of moral entrepreneur—as individuals and groups claiming the superiority of their values over others. Other moral crusades result from efforts to improve the importance, standing, and funding of bureaucracy as pointed out by Donald T. Dickson. Dickson explores how an army of illicit drug users was invented by the United States Bureau of Narcotics to expand its scope of operations by molding public and congressional opinion against drug use.[8] Examining the motivations of moral entrepreneurs may be particularly fruitful, for while they cloak themselves in moral wrappings that lend legitimacy, underlying this may be a considerable degree of self-interest.

In addition to those who engage in entrepreneurial efforts to create new deviance designations, there are other groups that historically have established their right to do so and seek to continue to expand their domain. Chief among these is the medical profession that has been accorded the right to define health and disease. In exercising this right, the worth of each practitioner is validated. As Eliot Freidson points out, "One of the greatest ambitions of the physician is to discover and describe a 'new' disease or syndrome and to be immortalized by having his name used to identify the disease." Medicine, then, is oriented to seeking out and finding illness, which is to say that it seeks to create social meanings of illness where that meaning or interpretation was lacking before. And insofar as illness is defined as something bad, to be eradicated or contained, medicine plays the role of what Becker calls the moral entrepreneur.[9]

A somewhat similar aspect of the social construction of reality through labeling is the process by which existing deviance designations take on new meanings. Old labels are not simply elaborated; they are redefined to fit within another nomenclature entirely. Freidson notes this trend when he writes that "Modern times are witness to the inclusion of more behavior under the concept of disease than ever before."[10] Conrad and Schneider, in examining the adoption of deviant behaviors as medical problems by the medical profession, refer to the process by which this occurs as the "medicalization of deviance." These authors propose a sequential model to account for the manner in which this shift in nomenclature and domain unfolds. In the first stage, "definition of behavior as deviant," existing definitions are in place, such as alcoholic, drug addict, but are vague and formless. The public view of these deviancies is that they result from others' weaknesses, whether it be an inability to resist temptation, inadequate self-control, or lacking sufficient character to resist falling prey to the corrupting influence of others.

The second stage is one of "medical discovery" that occurs when journal articles proclaim new diagnoses, thus providing definition to known deviancies. This part of the process occurs primarily in the academic or within the profession realm, falling short of reaching the public. The third stage, "claims-making," is the principle mover in the emergence of new deviance designations. Public claims are made about the "discovery" or success of the treatment by moral entrepreneurs who may be medical researchers or are involved administratively in handling one or another deviant population. Information, in highly dramatic form, begins to filter to the public that "recent medical discoveries" have shown that there is a significant physiological or biochemical difference between the alcoholic, the addict, or the criminal and the rest of us. The information may be presented in capsule form in Sunday newspaper magazines, in newscasts on television, or by a commentator speaking to us via radio.

Stage four, "legitimacy: securing medical turf," sees a shift in the arena to legislative committees and courtrooms where validation is sought in the body politic. Finally, the process moves to the final stage in which the medical deviance designation is institutionalized by being codified and bureaucratized.[11]

The medicalized deviances the authors explore include mental illness, alcoholism, opiate addiction, and a number of special problems of children including delinquency, hyperactivity, and child abuse. Other types of deviance in which efforts to medicalize have not been successful, including homosexuality and criminal behavior, are also examined. The latter two deviancies provide examples of the fact that the sequential model is not always successful in that the claims of one group can be contested by others. That is, there are groups, as in the case of homosexuals, who are capable of organizing and exerting pressure to deny the designation of illness and successfully fight it as a definition. Also, there are groups such as prison officials, state corrections departments and police associations that reject the proferred definition of criminals as being emotionally troubled and perhaps mentally ill. In the case of alcoholism, which has passed through the sequential model and has become medicalized, a significant portion of the population and the medical profession do not accept the definition as accurate or only give lip service to it.

At times, some groups are able to skip some of the intermediate steps in the sequential model proposed by Conrad and Schneider, probably due to the specialized nature of their domain and the relative weakness of competing groups. In psychiatry, the social construction of labels is facilitated through the development and dissemination of the American Psychiatric Association's diagnostic manual that has gone through two major revisions. The latest version, known as DSM-III, includes "a listing of the official code numbers and terms for all mental disorders recognized by APA (American Psychiatric Association) and also includes a comprehensive description of and specified diagnostic criteria for each category of disorder." The author goes on to point out, "The manual truly represents the most advanced developments in diagnosis, and as such it has generally been adopted for official use in mental health facilities throughout the country."[12] While many psychologists have opposed the codification of DMS-III because it medicalizes a vast array of habits and behaviors that were not included in DSM-II, their opposition is unlikely to halt its dissemination and use.

At times, new euphemisms are invented to label persons who are particularly troublesome to human service professionals and the underlying hostility to such individuals is barely concealed. For example, Workshop 50 of the 1982 annual meeting of the American Orthopsychiatric Association was publicized in the following manner in the official program announcement:

REVOLVING DOOR FAMILIES: TREATMENT DILEMMA,
BURN-OUT BURDEN AND SYSTEMS DRAIN

Revolving Door Families, as clinical entities are best noted by their repetitive, often inappropriate and non-productive appearance at medical and mental health care facilities. Focus is on etiology, and therapeutic, financial, organizational strains imposed by this (mis) use of treatment resources.

3. Proclaiming Labels in Mass Communication Media

A systematic investigation of the influence of the mass media is a very complex task that is beyond the scope of this discussion of the creation of labels. Thomas Scheff has touched on this matter in his exploration of the role of cultural stereotypes in the perpetuation of mental illness. Scheff shows how newspapers link mental illness and violence by reporting that "a rapist or murderer was once a mental patient" but seldom describe the positive accomplishments of former mental patients.[13] In this and other ways the media provide form and shape to the meaning of labels but do not, in effect, create them.

Morris Janowitz has traced the intellectual history of the study of the mass media and its impact on the population. He notes that "by means of press, radio, TV, films, books, magazines, etc., small specialized groups are able to create and disseminate symbolic content to a large, heterogeneous, and widely dispersed audience." Media experts are, in effect, influenced by their audience and audiences' responses, i.e. an interactive situation, but there is an "imbalance in influence and power" in which media specialists "overwhelmingly outweigh the contributions of the audience."[14] Janowitz goes on to explore the apparent preoccupation of television with themes of violence that has been the subject of at least 500 studies and a number of Congressional inquiries. The important trend he identifies "in popular culture content is the rise and persistence of violent themes" that appear "not in the public affairs coverage but in the popular culture and entertainment content." Janowitz speculates that "the long term effect has been to heighten projective (and accordingly suspicious) personality predispositions and defensive group affiliations."[15] A media generated construction of reality in which violence dominates the social scene is conducive to an increase in labeling since (a) labels serve to separate the "bad guys" from the "good guys" thereby adding order to our world; (b) violence is linked with existing but diffuse label designations such as "psychotic killer" and "crazed dope addict"; and (c) violence perpetrated against deviants is permissible once the recipient has been dehumanized with a highly negative label.

Recently the mass media has featured reports, articles, and in the case of television, semidocumentary offerings highlighting violent juvenile crime despite the fact that both the rate and incidence of serious juvenile offenses have decreased during the decade.[16] Words such as "observer" and "audience" are used frequently by labeling theorists to connote unusual attention and interpretation drawn to otherwise unmeaningful or insignificant happenings. Media handling transforms an occurrence into an event; it amplifies rather than creates, but this act may yield a qualitative difference in audience perspectives. Media reporting of crimes may lead people to believe they are unsafe, that criminal behavior is endemic, and thieves and muggers are all around them. Not only does crime tend to receive more than its share of attention in the media, but reports of increases in certain types of crime and general crime rates are at times skillfully utilized by police agencies and politicians to benefit their circumstances.[17]

Another way that the media contributes to the social construction of labels is through the reporting of claims, statements, and findings of researchers that are calculated to spark the public's imagination and draw attention to their "discoveries." New labels are frequently created in this manner, despite the fact that codification has not and may never occur. For example, research on the theory that there is a relationship between the XYY karyotype and crime, the extra chromosome makes for a "double" male, received extensive coverage in the media following a report that persons with the genetic characteristic appeared in greater than expected numbers in a single prison.[18] John Lofland suggests that through the influence of universal state education and mass communication, the population is becoming exposed to an increasing number of deviant categories in relatively short periods of time. While some categories, such as witches, seem to disappear, the psychiatric establishment has "vigorously disseminated conceptions of certain acts as criteria of various kinds of mental illness."[19] A national Sunday news magazine that provides a weekly quiz to entertain readers, offered a six statement "true or false" labeling test entitled "Are You Neurotic?" The test included such statements as, "most people have neurotic tendencies," and "it's easy for a person to determine the extent to which he is neurotic or well adjusted."[20] Each of the six answers includes partial citations of research performed by psychologists, psychiatrists, and other "specialists" that offer "proof" that a true or false answer to a particular question places a reader in the category of being neurotic. While it is doubtful that many people would take this seriously enough to label themselves, such information can be turned against others in an environment that breeds suspicion.

Claims that certain types of diet are implicated in causing juvenile delinquency, that viewing violence on television can contribute to disorder among youthful audiences, and that certain patterns in fingerprints can lead to the identification of latent criminals have been subject to recent research and subsequent media reportage. However, it should be noted, that the media frequently overgeneralize findings and fail to distinguish between correlation and causation, leaving the impression that more "facts" have been presented than actually have been discussed.

4. Organizations That are Responsible for Handling Deviants

In Chapter 1 it was pointed out that human service organizations play an important role in defining deviance. On the one hand, they define the putative deviant, providing form and substance to peoples' opinions or suspicions about others. On the other, they become a visible representation of an established order for the control of deviance. Mental hospitals are for the mentally ill and prisons are for the criminals among us. In these ways human service organizations transact social policy toward deviants that has been created elsewhere, by legislative bodies, United Way planning groups, and similar organizations. The impression one is left with is that these organizations are reactive, not proactive, and that undifferentiated types of deviants are brought to them for labeling. Only in part is this true. Many human service organizations play an active role in seeking out persons to be fitted with a label, for they engage in entrepreneurial activities. As Lofland notes,

> While such organizations may appear to be in the business of repressing or eliminating deviance, this is not the case at all. First and foremost their "job" is to find deviants to repress or change. In all of social life, a high

probability for the occurrence of a set of activities is best ensured by giving a set of others some interest in, and pay-off for, performing them. In the same way that profit in industrial manufacture ensures a flow of goods, the flow of imputations of pivotal deviance can be facilitated by paying people to spend a major portion of their time making them. As the number of imputational specialists increases in a society, it is likely that the number of people imputed as deviant will also increase.[21]

Modern times have seen an apt name given to organizations that locate deviants and broaden the meaning of deviance designations; they are case finding agencies. Two examples from among the many available are sufficient to illustrate the role these agencies play in creating deviance designations. First, the community mental health center, with its psychiatric dominance, has moved far beyond the traditional jurisdiction of psychiatry. As Conrad and Schneider observe: "The Domain . . . includes not only traditional mental illness conceptions, but alcoholism, drug addiction, children's school and behavior problems, predelinquency, bad marriages, job losses, and aging. Virtually any human problem could be addressed. . . . "[22] A second example is that of child abuse and its prevention. As a result of certain policy decisions the primary program that has evolved to "combat" child abuse consists of discovering parents who abuse their children. Richard J. Gelles identifies specialists who proffer the child abuser designation as "gatekeepers" who are "those individuals or agencies that operate as the main gatekeepers in the process of labeling and defining a child as abused and a caretaker as an abuser."[23] Casefinding, or locating persons who fit the label is a key role of these organizations. David Gil is quite critical of this singular approach to combatting child abuse and claims that a much greater number of children are victims of societal (rather than parental) forms of abuse such as poor education and inadequate medical services, poverty and its accompanying malnutrition, and physical abuse in schools and other child case institutions.[24] Instead, the child abuse reporting movement concentrates a major portion of its energy on locating battered children and labeling abusive parents.

The recent movement to place casefinding or gatekeeping specialists in other types of organizations such as social workers in factories and police in public schools is a response to a set of problems that may have the unintended consequence of ensuring that behavior which in the past was seen as a simple variant of normality will now be designated deviant. The discovery of deviants by all these organizations and specialists brings the social construction of labels to full circle. The claims of groups who have the power to create labels are proven. They and the media can now present data attesting to the volume of deviances newly discovered, and the public can attribute perceived disorder in the social structure to an emerging army of deviants.

PRIMARY AND SECONDARY DEVIANCE

In 1951, Edwin M. Lemert proposed a distinction between engaging in occasional nonconforming or deviant behavior and a continuing pattern of deviance in which the nonconformity becomes a central fact of life for the individual. He distinguished primary deviation, a violation of the norms, from secondary deviation whereby the actor, as a consequence of societal reaction and subsequent adjustment of self to this reaction, becomes committed to a "deviant career."[25]

In Lemert's view the actor, a primary deviant, has a new set of definitions prescribing his identity thrust upon him with which he must somehow reckon in order to stabilize his life. The typical definitional process that occurs is one in which labeling forces a change in the individual's self-perception. Labeling, in this way, becomes the social process that transforms one conception of self into another, or put another way, labeling can instigate the shift from a normal identity to a deviant one.[26] Thus, occasional misbehavior in school, a primary deviation, does not lead the pupil to define himself as bad, or even to deny that he is until deviant motives are imputed by the teacher. When this imputation occurs in public, such as the classroom setting, and is denigrating and demeaning, other pupils may follow the teacher's lead and perpetuate the name-calling in gym class, the lunchroom, and on the playground. Should the pupil's burgeoning reputation be spread to other teachers, regardless of any overt acts on his part, his behavior in the future will be more closely observed with suspicion. This new public image may lead to a reconstitution of his self-concept, as was seen in the example of Mike at the beginning of this chapter.

The distinction between primary and secondary deviance is not always an easy one to comprehend as we think of case examples, since unseen or psychological processes are occurring alongside visible social ones. At what point does the young woman who enjoys many sexual partners and accepts gifts from these men begin to regard herself as a "common whore"? Arriving at this self-appraisal may depend upon who she associates with, her circle of friends, the circumstances under which the liaisons occur and their frequency, the reactions of the men and the degree of knowledge and attitudes of the neighbors. The occurrence or development of secondary deviance is dependent upon the nature of the social reaction, which varies tremendously, and the actor's perception of that reaction to his or her primary deviant behavior. Controlled environments in which to examine these concepts are difficult if not impossible to locate.

A study by Joseph W. Eaton and Robert J. Weil, however, provides a good example of a relatively isolated community in which persons who are mentally ill remain primary deviants and maintain an adequate adjustment to prevailing social norms. The investigators studied the Hutterites who are a homogeneous, relatively self-contained community of people of German origins living in the Dakotas, Montana, and extending into Manitoba, Canada. Over time their society has appealed to investigators because of an apparent ease of living of members, a high degree of community responsibility for individuals, and "economic security from the womb to the tomb" that leaves the group "free from many of the tensions of the American melting pot culture." As a consequence of their benign culture and an apparent lack of stress befalling the individual, the Hutterites were thought to be "almost immune to mental disorders." Eaton and Weil found that "on the surface it seemed that the Hutterites did enjoy extraordinary freedom from mental illness." They did not find a single Hutterite in a mental hospital nor did records reveal any community member having been admitted to one. Upon closer examination, however, the investigators found Hutterites "who either had active symptoms of a mental disorder or had recovered from such an illness."

While the investigators observed that the rate of mental illness was low in comparison to other populations, there is ample evidence of its existence.[27]

Mental illness as a primary deviation is present among the Hutterites but can the same be said about secondary deviance? Are there individuals occupying a role that is disparaged, wherein the occupant of the role is isolated and shunned by community members and not only continues to act strangely but does so increasingly? Apparently not. Eaton and Weil note the response of the Hutterite culture to mental illness. "Although it does not prevent mental disorders, it provides a highly therapeutic atmosphere for their treatment. The onset of a symptom serves as a signal to the entire community to demonstrate support and love for the patient. . . . All patients are looked after by the immediate family. They are treated as ill rather than 'crazy'. They are encouraged to participate in the normal life of their family and community. . . . "[28] The following can be surmised from this study:

1. Mental illness is present among the Hutterites.
2. The social group reacts to mental illness benignly and integrates the mentally ill individual into the community.
3. A deviant career is not socially prescribed for the mentally ill individual.
4. The community's response to primary deviance fails to produce secondary deviance.*

THE LABELING PERSPECTIVE

In examining several theories regarding deviant behavior in preceding chapters we observed that the chief concern of these theories was to explain either the original source of deviant behavior or to account for its manifestation in a particular person. Most, but not all of these theories, assume a common cultural value system or at best a widespread consensus in society about norms and values. If shared values are assumed, then it becomes a fairly

---

*For a thorough discussion of the Hutterites as both a movement and a community, see John A. Hostetler, *Hutterite Society* (Baltimore: Johns Hopkins University Press, 1977).

simple matter to discover the ways in which deviants differ from nondeviants. For example, if an intact and stable family system is a positive value, then delinquency can be attributed to disrupted family life since a significant proportion of youth in juvenile training schools come from broken homes. Or, one may study delinquents longitudinally to determine when the family was first disrupted and compare this with the first recorded signs of deviant behavior.

Labeling theory presents a different starting place. It concentrates not on the origins of deviant behavior but on the consequences of identifying a person as deviant. For the Hutterites there are minimal negative social consequences in being identified and treated as sick (mentally ill). For other citizens in the United States, being labeled mentally ill can mean a lowering of social status, loss of employment or occupational career, regulation by mental health agencies, and tenuous relations with others.

Labeling theory receives its name from its major concern with the dynamics of socially defining particular activities or people as deviant. It is not a single theoretical position but a collection of themes and viewpoints presented by sociologists who take exception to the use of psychological, biological, and structural theories used to explain why people deviate. Where values are at issue labeling theory does not assume consensus but rather diversity and conflict. Where people are being stamped as inferior or morally unfit the name callers are seen as expressing value judgments. They are posing one set of values as superior to others.

What is the relevance of labeling theory for human service professionals? First, social workers, psychologists, and psychiatrists have been accorded the right and often the responsibility by society to label people and are therefore labeling professionals. There are few contexts and circumstances in which the human service professional does not label before embarking on a course of treatment. Also, they manage and work in human service organizations that frequently produce results quite different from those intended. For example, persons who work in mental hospitals talk about patients becoming overdependent upon the setting, fearful of leaving, and unable to make decisions for themselves: they have become "institutionalized." Children in public schools who were earmarked for special education classes and schools never seemed to return to the normal track, thereby inadvertently having opportunities sealed off.

Then too, human service professionals often appear to be unaware of the effect of their label-dispensing in exacerbating the very condition they seek to remedy. We shall say more about these matters in Chapter 5 when we examine the individual's reaction to being labeled.

The labeling perspective views social control as a causal force in the creation and perpetuation of deviant behavior. It represents a view among sociologists that those who study deviance by searching for factors that deviants have in common are in error and that a central fact about deviance is its creation by society. Social groups create deviance by making the rules whose infraction constitutes deviance and then applying these rules throughout the population of rule breakers in a selective manner.[29] The processes involved in rule making and rule enforcing become, in this view, an important subject to be examined; or, as John I. Kitsuse states, "I propose to shift the focus of theory and research from the forms of deviant behavior to the processes by which persons come to be defined as deviant by others."[30]

The terms *society, social groups,* and *audiences* are used somewhat ambiguously throughout the literature but labeling theorists appear to be referring to at least three types of groups that have an impact upon rule makers and rule breakers.

1. Those persons and groups who come into interpersonal contact with specific rule violators: family, neighbors, fellow employees, employers, and passersby who seek to protect, ignore, shun, disapprove, or verbally attack the individual deviant. Their action field is primarily within the interpersonal affective realm; they rarely engage in collective action but respond expressively to observed deviant behavior. They consist of both intimate and distant audiences.

2. Various pressure groups and lobbies who respond collectively to apparent rule violations and exercise power by influencing rule makers. Rule makers, in this context, consist of legislators, public officials, and department heads who rely, to an extent, on the goodwill of the public to maintain their positions. Antiabortion, antigambling, and antipornography pressure groups, by influencing legislation, contribute both directly and indirectly to the creation of the rules.

These groups also consist of human service organizations and professionals who "discover" and stake claims to new forms of deviance such as child abuse, spouse abuse, and learning disorders of children. Their action fields are the various political arenas; their goals are values dominance, policy determination, and program implementation.

3. *Those persons, groups, and structures that enforce the rules, such as police, court officers, teachers, and agency personnel.* They impact directly on deviants; they apprehend, manage, treat, or control rule violators. Their action field consists of interventions directed at the deviant in order to effect some sort of changed behavior. Naturally, these groups may overlap. Enforcers may engage in lobbying activity, and pressure group members may come into interpersonal contact with deviants.

Each of these groups is active in social control in that they have a stake in system maintenance that is threatened by deviants. They are also values expressive. By their actions and inactions, they support the preservation of existing values over the preferences and behavior of the deviant. The deviant is seen not only as a rule violator, but as someone who is challenging, deliberately or inadvertently, the values underlying the rules.

A pivotal point in the labeling perspective is that identification as a deviant has salient consequences for the individual, both symbolic and real. The individual must not only deal with the specific consequences of being labeled deviant in terms of penalties exacted by those who enforce the rules but must also come to grips with a new-found identity. Definition as a deviant may lead to deviant careers. Denial of deviance becomes more difficult, insistence that one is a good person becomes tenuous, and the separation of self from the stereotypic images of persons who "do that kind of thing" can become impossible through constant reminders provided by the doubts of others.

Some confusion and misinterpretation has resulted from critics viewing the preceding broad and general concepts as being deterministic. One critic of the theory has assumed that labeling or social reaction is presented as being "the source of chronic rule breaking."[31] Labeling theorists do not view social reaction as the only source of career deviance or as inevitably leading to it. It is, however, the one source they wish to study since they believe it has been neglected and is of considerable importance. Career deviance, for example, extended homosexual conduct may have any number of sources and there is a vast literature on the etiology of homosexuality. Labeling theorists' interest extends to the circumstances involved in the transition of a homosexual identity involving the actor and his or her audience. Etiology or original causation is of secondary interest.[32]

It should be useful at this point to examine the fundamentals of labeling theory. The tenets that follow are organized sequentially to depict a process that flows from engaging in a deviant act to becoming a deviant person. Labeling theorists have differing views about the relative importance of each stage in the process but nearly all would agree that the encounter between rule breakers and audiences creates special problems for non-conforming persons.

CENTRAL TENETS OF LABELING THEORY

1. Deviance, or nonconforming behavior arises out of diverse sources and circumstances. Explanations for these events cannot be subsumed under some all-embracing theory.[33] Attention to etiological formulations has not only produced a different theory proposing the origins of each disorder but has also led to the generation of multiple and conflicting theories for most. Lemert despairs of this approach and asserts that "there are almost as many theories as there are writers on these subjects. This has been occasioned in no small way by the preoccupation with the origins of behavior and by the fallacy of confusing original causes with effective causes."[34] An original cause, for example, of a delinquent act by a youth can be identified as a disrupted family situation in which he was abandoned as a child. During ensuing years he was moved from foster home to foster home and then to an institution. An effective cause would invoke those more recent circumstances of the youth, interactions at school, or the specific events that led up to the delinquent act, which can be traced directly to the delinquency.

While labeling theorists disagree on the importance of original causes, their main concern is with processes involved in the instigation and perpetuation of continuing deviant behavior among persons that may have little or nothing at all to do with the origins of the initial deviant act. They emphasize the interactional, situational, and process features of deviant behavior, not its origins.

2. *Deviant acts alone do not make deviants.* "Deviations are not significant until they are organized subjectively and transformed into active roles and become the social criteria for assigning status."[35] Most of us commit seriously deviant acts at some times during our lives. Some of us do so continuously but the deviance that is committed remains secret; it is undetected by others. It is definitions by others that cause deviant careers by generating the symbolic processes that define actors negatively.[36] Indeed, there are many secret deviants, but their lives are segmented into diverse roles, most of which are conforming. They are seen as normal persons by most audiences with whom they interact. "Nearly all [labeling theorists] agree that those nonconformists who are singled out by the police, mental health personnel, or other social audiences face adjustment problems concerning spoiled identity that hidden deviants do not encounter."[37]

As Cohen notes, "A deviant act, if undetected, or ignored, might not be repeated. On the other hand, others might react to it by publicly defining the actor as a delinquent, a fallen woman, a criminal. These definitions ascribe to [the individual] a social role, change his public image, and activate a set of appropriate responses. These responses may include exclusion from avenues of legitimate opportunity formerly open to him, and thus enhance the relative attractiveness of the illegitimate."[38]

Current concerns in many cities with "sin strips," areas in which pornographic bookstores and massage parlors are concentrated, demonstrate that a considerable traffic in hidden or secret deviancy exists. Presumably these establishments are frequented by ordinary citizens who enjoy positive social roles and statuses in their communities while their "deviance" remains undetected.

3. *Deviance theorists focus on formal or official labeling due to its potent effects on deviants that is not shared by informal labeling.* As Davis observes, "While families, peer groups and occupational associates may be highly instrumental in shaping deviant outcomes, formal organizations serve as a particularly potent force in

activating, propelling, or imposing a deviant self-concept."[39] Official labeling is said to affect negatively the individual rule breaker by (a) establishing an individual's public identity as deviant; (b) creating, maintaining and, at times, disseminating files and information about him; (c) marking him for surveillance and supervision by agencies of social control; and (d) permitting further regulation without resort to due process protections.

Informal labeling by audiences with whom the individual comes into contact can have telling effects. Indeed, concern with what others think of us, or what they might think of us were we to deviate, is a basic element of social control. Informal labels, however, in contrast with formal labels, generally have a number of characteristics that modify or reduce their potency. One characteristic is their diffuseness or nonspecificity in that they generally fail to lead to clear role differentiations. A woman may be informally labeled "loose," a youth may be seen as a "troublemaker," and someone may be called "crazy," but they are also seen as persons who fulfill other normal social roles. In addition, informal labels are opinions, not facts, and can more easily be contested by others in the audience or the deviant individual. Aberrations can be seen as transitory, results of unusual situational pressures, or compensated for by other positive attributes and role performances. A heavy drinker who is also a "good" husband and father is viewed far differently from someone formally labeled an alcoholic.

Another distinction between the two types of labels is that other persons generally make accommodations to acquaintances who are informally labeled. While the reasons for this phenomenon are generally unknown, a social psychology textbook suggest a universal "positivity bias" that "reflects a particular leniency we have in evaluating our fellow human beings: based on the assumption that others are similar to us."[40] The behavior of persons who have been informally labeled may be ignored, excused, or taken for granted by others in order to preserve existing patterns of relationship.[41] These types of responses are useful in normalizing potentially uncomfortable interpersonal interactions. On the other hand, official labels, those dispensed by various agencies and social control structures, validate the vague perception that the individual's behavior is markedly different, true deviance and not just a variation of normalcy. Awareness of the label leads the audience to impugn a master status to the individual, be it prostitute, criminal, alcoholic, or mentally ill; and all other statuses, father, engineer, and the like, recede in significance.

4. *One of the ways an individual gains a deviant self-image is through labeling.* The shift in focus is from the social reaction of the audience and labelers to the perceptions of the actor being labeled. Whereas prior to labeling the actor can maintain to himself and others that the norm violations engaged in were alien to his or her true self, the possibility becomes far more remote once the label has been applied. One possible consequence is an altered identity in the actor, necessitating a reconstitution of self.[42]

People do not ordinarily think of themselves as deviants even though they occasionally engage in deviant behavior. They will attempt to justify their behavior as accidental, a temporary aberration, or a consequence of undue pressures or admit to a lesser degree of guilt, such as noting, "it was the first time." These rationalizations generally prove ineffective following formal labeling, and the actor must somehow deal with his or her new public image. He or she may be motivated to do what is necessary to regain a conventional image and cease the deviant behavior entirely. Or, for any number of reasons, he or she may not. The person may, in the face of overwhelming evidence and public denunciation, accept the label as truly representing his or her identity. This is a form of self-labeling that should not be understood as an invariable result of social reaction nor does eventual commitment to a deviant career necessarily require such processes.[43] Instead, the processes enhance the likelihood of these outcomes.

The interactional theme imbedded in labeling theory suggests that the additional ingredients in determining outcomes of these social processes are the actor's choice, proclivities, and, perhaps, problem-solving skills. But most important is the actor's perception of the situation, the meaning it has for him or her. Lemert is very specific on this point and makes reference to the youth who appears before the juvenile court. "The ancient ceremonial there may strike him with awe and fear, but if nothing much happens as a consequence, the memory fades or is retrospectively rationalized."[44]

5. *According to this formulation of a process theory, two things are*

necessary for a deviant career to unfold. The actor must be both labeled and stigmatized. Stigmatization, according to Lemert, "describes a process attaching visible signs of moral inferiority to persons, such as invidious labels, marks, brands, or publicly disseminated information: the 'prevailing consequences' of the labeling procedure."[45] Using Lemert's example of an event that may not be stigmatizing in itself, a youth's appearance before the juvenile court, the process can be extended through a not so hypothetical occurrence in which the court social worker seeks to gather more information. The youth's school is called to find out how he is getting along in that setting. While school personnel may not have noted any problems, they have now been alerted to the fact that the youth's reputation may not be quite what they thought it was. The youth is now to be watched more closely at school and minor incidents and acts are interpreted in a new light, the behavior of a delinquent. Stigmatization has been initiated.

Stigmatization, by and large, is a collective process carried forward in organizational and community context. Some organizations stigmatize through rigid rules and limitations such as the parole agency that requires that permission be sought by the deviant before he can change his residence, purchase a car, travel out-of-state, or get married. Other organizations, such as mental health agencies, may deny the patient the tranquilizing drugs he seeks unless he complies with the therapist's expectations regarding participation in other aspects of the organization's program.

Stigmatization, then, has at least two consequences that can steer persons toward deviant careers. First, it restricts the stigmatized individual's options for returning to normalcy. Acceptance by other "normals" or conventional society is curtailed and replaced by reactions ranging from mild distrust to outright rejection. Friends seem to disappear, and jobs are more difficult to find. Second, the actor must take stock of these new events and determine what sort of person he or she really is. Others are no longer reacting to the individual but to his or her label, or, as Davis puts it, "the deviant identity alone becomes real, having a life-force that transcends the individuals possessing it."[46]

As a concept advanced by labeling theorists, the meaning of stigma is diffuse and vague. On the one hand, it is presented as a mark or brand accompanying a label dispensed by one agency or another which serves to discredit deviants; mental patients, special education students, and parolees are provided as examples. On the other hand, stigma is a subjective state, a recognition by the actor that his identity has changed, or been revealed, and yet he continues to attempt to conceal it. Former mental patients and prisoners may deliberately omit their discredited past on application forms for jobs or college admission. Persons who have been in treatment with psychologists, psychiatrists, or social workers are very cautious about to whom they impart this information. The subjective side of stigma, the actor's awareness of the discrediting characteristic, takes center stage creating extreme sensitivity to interpersonal encounters and perhaps, a crisis in identity.

Actions by deviants to hide or disguise what has happened to them through labeling are seen as efforts to avoid yet a third aspect of stigma, the punishment it draws from audiences. Such punishments consist largely of rejection, exclusion, and discrimination in diverse contexts. Deviant persons find that they are ostracized from some groups and ridiculed by some people. The pains of stigma, especially the punishment aspect, are frequently sufficient to have the actor cease the deviant activity. Furthermore, public awareness of these pains performs a social function in deterring others from engaging in that type of behavior. In those contexts in which the individual cannot avoid or conceal stigma, the commitment to conventional norms and behavior is weakened and the passageways to a deviant career become more attractive.

6. *The social reaction to the deviant individual is one mechanism that can act to stabilize a deviant role and create secondary, or career, deviance.* Secondary deviance "refers to a special class of socially defined responses which people make to problems created by the societal reaction to their deviance."[47] The career concept is many sided. It calls to mind a social status derived from an occupation by which persons are identified, such as engineer, nurse, or teacher. Such careers typically achieve a central importance in the actor's life. They may account for whom the individual associates with, what he reads, how he votes, and his general perspectives about the world. Finally, one is likely to be ushered into a career through a ceremony, be it graduation from professional school, a gift of a set

of tools by one's family, or being "sworn in" to the police department. In an analogous fashion, the deviant is labeled and provided a new social status in a judgement ceremony, be it a trial or a diagnosis.

Howard Becker expands upon the evolution of secondary deviance by stressing "career contingencies," steps or factors that are followed or occur in sequence with the final state being movement into an organized deviant group.[48] Erving Goffman speculates on the "moral" aspects of the career of mental patients, particularly noting the sequence of changes entailed in the actor's self–other adjustments during phases of mental hospitalization.[49] Career is a mainspring of the labeling approach for it designates the turning point between random, noncommital deviant acts and a deviant identity organized around these acts. Its precedents include discovery, confrontation, and judgement by community members, taking on a new status and the necessary self-adjustments these processes require.[50]

Both social reaction and career contingencies, however, are highly variable, as it is individual motivation. Cohen elaborates further on these contingencies by noting that social reaction can also open up legitimate opportunities. Almost yearly newspapers report on a man in a small town caught stealing food. The police investigate further and discover that he is unemployed, has four children and a wife at home, the home being an unheated trailer or decaying house, and that they've been eating stale bread for a week. Offers of money and jobs pour in. Second, the social reaction may close off legitimate opportunities as in the misbehaving student being expelled from school or the shoplifting bank teller being fired from her job. Third, the social reaction may open up illegitimate opportunities or at least make them more attractive to pursue.[51]

The entire sequence leading to secondary deviance has been summarized by Lemert as follows:

(a) primary deviation; (b) social penalties; (c) further primary deviation; (d) stronger penalties and rejections; (e) further deviation, perhaps with hostilities and resentment beginning to focus upon those doing the penalizing; (f) crisis reached in the tolerance quotient, expressed in formal action by the community stigmatizing of the deviant; (g) strengthening of the deviant conduct as a reaction to the stigmatizing and penalties;

(h) ultimate acceptance of deviant social status and efforts of adjustment on the basis of the associated role.[52]

7. *In the view of many labeling theorists, human service organizations play a key role in seeking to resolve problems of deviance and in so doing produce results quite different from those intended.* Some of these organizations, such as courts and public schools, that dispense labels routinely are instrumental in the creation of deviants. Others are responsible for managing formal deviant statuses; for example, probation agencies and after-care units for the mental patient released from an institution. Some, such as the mental hospital, may do both.

The following are organizational activities and efforts that are thought to promote career deviance and enhance stigma:

a. Formal label designations are almost always dispensed through organizations. These designations, because they are authoritative pronouncements, are virtually impossible for the individual to successfully deny both within the organization and the person's milieu. Furthermore, they are likely to persist over time, and it is rare that these designations can be overcome through the individual's efforts.

b. Through their diagnostic processes human service organizations evaluate and designate the worth of each client, determine degrees of willfulness and malleability and ultimately, the moral character of the individual to be served. Operatives within these organizations act on the broader social definitions revolving around perceived moral failings of deviant types and reify them with each individual client. Organizational operatives attempt to force a self-image on the person that is congruent with organizational images.

c. The use of position-derived power by operatives within these organizations to force certain desired behaviors upon clients reduces the individuals' freedom of choice and autonomy and creates greater alienation or, conversely, dependence.

d. Individuals labeled by these organizations undergo status transformations. They become mentally impaired (a school label), convicted rapist (a court label), hebephrenic schizophrenic (a mental hospital or community mental health center label), that is, they become their label. These labels denote both new and different identities. Once labeled the persons who are in the care of such organizations are viewed by the public as possessing defective attributes.

e. Self-serving activities by organizational operatives whereby they seek to protect themselves or enhance their positions at the expense of clients such as extended stays in the mental hospital by "dangerous" patients, excessive and indiscriminate use of tranquilizer drugs, and lengthy detention of juveniles who have been involved in minor offenses.

f. The failure of the organization, following a course of treatment, to effectively eliminate the label from adhering to the person. While the public rarely questions the correctness of the label when it is originally dispensed, there seems to be a profound distrust of organizational operatives' judgement that the person is fit, that he has been corrected, following discharge or release. In a sense, organizations have the ability to dispense labels but lack the ability to remove them from the public's consciousness.

Identification of these seven central tenets of labeling theory should not lead one to the conclusion that all must be present to cause career deviance or that they must proceed in exact order to produce that result. People and the situations they find themselves in are simply too variable to yield a single result from any one set of circumstances. What these tenets identify is an interactional perspective that "focuses on the open-ended, situational construction of reality, in which meanings ... arise and are defined and altered by participants in the course of action. The self, as a social object, is an ever-emerging product, and not, as other psychologies claim, a set of traits."[53] Labeling theory is by no means a complete theory but serves instead to pose a set of issues or sensitizing concepts useful in the study of deviance.[54] It serves to identify the dual focus most useful in understanding deviance, the interaction of the individual and society.

STEREOTYPES IN THE CREATION OF DEVIANTS

A stereotype is a popular image, a picture that is brought to mind when we hear about other persons and groups. We have images of what judges look like, how entertainers enjoy themselves, and how mentally ill people behave. We have racial, religious, ethnic, and gender-related stereotypes as well as images of what adolescents and the elderly are like. These images, what Goode refers to as "mental cartoons of other people," become public stereotypes when large numbers of people share similar views of others.[55]

One of the reasons for the success of con artists who engage in scams in order to fleece unwary citizens is their ability to convey a public, nondeviant stereotype through which they attract the trust of their victims. There are many positive stereotypes that we learn through childhood socialization and lifelong exposure to the mass media. Firemen are stereotyped as helpful, airline pilots as skillful, and nurses as kind. As a consequence, we are positively disposed toward such persons.

There are also negative stereotypes that are learned in much the same way as those that are positive. Sociologists who are concerned with the effects of racial and ethnic discrimination and prejudice have viewed stereotyping uniformly as negative in character. Stereotypes contain, in the case of those held about minorities, "noisy" attributes that are false or exaggerated elements within a category.[56] These "noisy" attributes, wherein blacks are regarded as hostile and perhaps criminal; Hispanics are seen as lazy and (alternately) volatile, and Jews are imputed to be stingy, predispose people negatively toward these groups. Second, positive traits are ignored or reinterpreted to be negative as Robert Merton has noted: "Did [Abraham] Lincoln work far into the night? This testifies that he was industrious, resolute, perseverant, and eager to realize his capacities to the full. Do the out-group Jews or Japanese keep the same hours? This only bears witness to their sweatshop mentality, their ruthless undercutting of American standards, their unfair competitive practices."[57] Ostensibly, in Merton's example, Lincoln, Jews, and Japanese engage in similar behavior. As a result of stereotyping, the motivation and social value of the behavior, when practiced by Jews or Japanese, is turned completely around. Interpretation of the meaning of the behavior as opposed to its objective features becomes crucial. The stereotype persists in the face of contrary evidence, that is, a cluster of fixed ideas takes precedence over personal observation that may challenge these ideas.

Observations by sociologists that people are predisposed by stereotypes suggest that achieving changes in public attitudes towards minority groups is no simple task. The difficulty is that positive traits observed in people who have been negatively stereotyped are rationalized negatively by others. The introduction of new information, no matter how accurate, is insufficient. An additional difficulty is the salience of negative traits or the "negativity effect." In discussing affiliation theory, Freedman, Sears, and Carlsmith cite the "negativity effect" as one in which: "positive and negative traits are not treated exactly alike [by audiences]. Although people seem to average the traits they hear about to arrive at a complete impression, they weigh negative information more heavily than they do positive information. That is, a negative trait affects an impression more than does a positive trait. . . . It follows that a positive impression is easier to change than a negative one."[58]

There are many parallels between ethnic and racial stereotypes and those applied to deviants, for categories of deviant behavior are also stereotypes. They serve to identify rule violators as members of groups who possess common negative characteristics. We each have stereotypes of criminals, drug addicts, and retarded adults as well as images of welfare recipients, divorced women, and the blind. J. L. Simmons, in his study of stereotyping, utilized interviewing techniques previously developed for studying attitudes toward ethnic minorities in order to explore stereotypes that people hold about deviants. He found an extremely high correlation between intolerance toward people in deviant categories and intolerance toward minorities.[59]

Stereotypes, as social categories, are in place long before we ever come into personal contact with deviants. Many are introduced during childhood socialization as symbols of what will happen when we break the rules and serve as generally effective elements in achieving social control. "Laws against such acts as homicide, drug use, assault, robbery, and embezzlement do not prevent their occurrence on a broad scale. Prevention, instead, is a function of individual traits that are 'built into' the personality at an early age when children are taught that certain kinds of activities are right or wrong."[60]

Stereotypes are instrumental in the creation of deviants; deviant acts alone are insufficient. More than thirty years ago Edwin Sutherland published his study of white-collar crime in which a vast array of criminal offenses committed by businessmen were analyzed. While most of these offenses were criminal, not civil offenses under the law, the public reaction was as if no crime had been committed.[61] Neither the corporations involved nor their responsible officers were invested with deviant characteristics. The public images of the corporations were not significantly damaged, and their officers continued to be respected citizens of their communities.[62] The study presented by Sutherland indicates that no negative public stereotype existed for white-collar criminals at that time. Nor has the situation changed that much to this present day. We know, however, that people convicted of other offenses, particularly what has become known as "street crimes" do fit the popular stereotype and are seen as being deviant. The negative public stereotype serves to mark the person as being distinctly different in terms of motivation and character from the rest of us. Negative public stereotypes are agreed-upon categories reserved for certain persons and not others.

There appears to be a tendency among people to join two different types of stereotypes, those pertaining to ethnic, racial, and other minorities and those related to deviant categories. For example, the stereotype about black men being lazy, unwilling to obtain or hold jobs is coupled with blacks' involvement in crime, especially in the larger cities of the Northeast and Midwest. In these same cities many people hold the stereotype that "welfare mothers" are predominantly black. While arrest and welfare rates may be higher for blacks than whites, the stereotype persists despite the fact that most blacks populate neither category. While the processes at work are undoubtedly very complex, the effect is readily apparent. To a considerable extent persons who populate deviant categories tend to be lower class, poor, and minority group members. They are far more likely to be seen, labeled, and processed as deviants and rejected by others.

There is a prevalent belief that the act of stereotyping is negatively associated with the achieved educational levels of people. We are prone to believe that the more ignorant people are the more likely they are to stereotype. This view is, of course, a stereotype about uneducated people. Stereotypes are social categories that are useful to all of us in coding a complex world. We simply cannot do without them. As people become more educated they trade old stereotypes for new ones. We would all like to believe that our new stereotypes are better informed, less biased, and more accurate, but this is not always the case. Stereotypes, new or old, are problematic since they overestimate within-group similarities and between-group differences, and they tend to be unresponsive to objective evidence.[63]

Simmons' study of the prevalance of stereotyping found that a fair amount of agreement existed about who was deviant and the negative traits such types of persons hold in common. He also found that a majority of even the most highly educated group in his study "expressed unequivocally negative stereotypes toward most or all of the deviant types." Adulterers, homosexuals, political radicals, and marijuana smokers were seen as deviant and as possessing associated negative traits by the highly educated group. However, a "secondary stereotype" of psychiatric interpretation was added; the highly educated appeared to soften negative and rejecting attitudes toward deviants through reference to psychiatric explanations in their stereotyping. As Simmons notes however, the more highly educated were simply more subtle in their stereotyping.[64]

An interesting paradox concerning public policies relating to the disciplining of children seems to have roots in how people stereotype one another and how legislators act on these stereotypes. Michigan Public Act 238 (1975) requires teachers to report bruises found on children that may have been inflicted by their parents. Michigan Public Act 451 (1976) permits teachers to inflict similar physical punishment on these and other children. The requirement for teachers to report bruises appears to be based on a stereotype of a parent wantonly beating a child, that is, child abuse. Administration of similar punishment by a teacher connotes a stereotype of dispassionate administration of discipline.

MEDICALIZED STEREOTYPES

Twenty years ago few people would have thought of compulsive gambling as a disease. The behavior of weak-willed persons perhaps, but not disease. Yet today, compulsive gambling is gaining recognition as an addictive disease; an affliction similar to alcoholism and drug addiction.

The expanding role of medicine as an institution has led to a situation in which medical care providers are increasingly called upon to deal with social problems. A textbook on the social dimensions of medical care identifies opposite positions regarding this development:

> The complex issue of whether or to what extent we are "overmedicalizing" many social problems (defining them as illness or disease and turning to medicine for their prevention, treatment, or cure) is one that disturbs many contemporary observers of American society. One simplistic view is that the medical care industry is essentially imperialistic and seeks to extend the borders of its influence and offer pronouncements and treatments for a wide variety of social ills including hyperactive children, substance use, and marital disharmony. Another view asserts that in the vacuum of human services aimed at dealing with such problems, medicine has been invited, perhaps dragged in, to deal with problems no other institutions are willing or able to deal with.[65]

A natural consequence of the medicalization of social problems is an increase in medical stereotypes wherein deviations from normative behavior are attributed to illness. Conrad and Schneider refer to this as the "medicalization of deviance." Organized medicine has asserted a claim that a wide variety of deviances are, in actuality, illnesses that should or do fall within the province of medicine. These authors are not referring to scientific or medical breakthroughs in the etiology of illnesses that were previously attributed to possession by devils as in epilepsy or to being cursed as in leprosy. Instead they propose that medical care providers have identified a range of troublesome behavior, such as alcoholism, homosexuality, and criminal actions as being the result of underlying illness.[66] According to this reasoning, diet deficiencies may cause delinquency in children, alcoholism is a physiological problem, and homosexuality is a mental deviation of sorts. Social judgements involving the imputation of "badness," a phenomenon of will, are replaced by medical stereotypes that impute causes beyond the control of the deviant.

One must ask, however, whether this shift in etiology has produced any change in stereotyping or the negative consequences that accrue to the person from it? As Conrad and Schneider note: "Can we think of any illness designations that are positive judgments or any illness conditions that are viewed as desirable states? Common sense also tells us that an entity labeled an illness or disease is considered undesirable."[67] Therefore medical stereotypes, like racial and ethnic stereotypes, tend to be negative in character.

There are at least three additional problems presented by this fairly recent, but very pervasive, shift toward medical stereotyping of deviants:

1. *They tend to become viewed as fact rather than theory by the public.* Medical stereotypes, like all stereotypes are theories about categories. They are supposed to be arrived at through the scientific method involving rules for concept formation, conduct of observations and experiments, and validation of hypotheses by observations or experiments. As a consequence, medical stereotypes are not subject to corrective efforts by advertising campaigns and other media pursuits that seek to educate the public regarding "false" stereotypes as we have seen in enlightening television presentations dealing with racial and religious intolerance and understanding mental illness. Second, some medical stereotypes may have evolved on the basis of tradition rather than through scientific methods but are utilized by professionals as if they are facts. Alex Kaplan, for example, notes that some of the categories in DSM–III, such as schizophrenia and affective organic mental disorders, result from scientific studies while others such as personality and sexual disorders are included "on the basis of tradition with the hope that by defining them with greater precision than

was previously done, further validity studies will justify their inclusion."[68] If Kaplan is correct, the DSM–III consists of labels that are facts (scientifically arrived at) and stereotypes that are theories but in actual practice, all will be treated as facts at least as far as diagnosis and billings for psychiatric treatment are concerned. Patients' records will variously contain both facts and theories, and who is to tell the difference between them?

2. *The belief that medical techniques can cure social problems.* The penetration and proliferation of medical stereotypes into the realm of social problems creates an aura that encourages people to believe that profound societal problems can be resolved through scientific breakthroughs, i.e., "magic bullets". Comments like "we are living in a pathological society" and "The economy is sick" are metaphors that invoke the belief that magical cures are possible. People come to believe that new cures for juvenile delinquency and overly aggressive children are possible and fall prey to professional hucksters who appear with programs promising no less than cures. One consequence of medical stereotyping in the social problem realm is to deflect attention away from the systemic sources of broadscale societal issues and problems.

3. *The use of medicalized stereotypes by nonmedical groups and professionals.*

This third problem has some overlap with the preceding two. Either through overzealousness or desperation, stereotypes are applied to problematic people who are said to resemble other label bearers or almost fit existing label categories. Children who violate conduct norms in the public schools are particularly vulnerable to this sort of stereotyping. Peter Schrag and Diane Divoky argue against the widespread practice of designating children learning disabled and as experiencing minimal brain dysfunction (M.B.D.) by public school personnel.[69] Indeed, there are known conditions such as Down's and Klinefelter's syndromes that may significantly impede learning in children, and the resulting frustration can lead to behavioral problems. What should be questioned is the practice by school personnel of suspecting that there are myriad other instances in which minimal brain dysfunction cannot be demonstrated or established due to the inadequacy of present diagnostic tools.[70] Frequently, children who are subject to these suspicions are treated as if minimal brain dysfunction exists. There can be three sets of consequences to this:

a. Misdiagnosis occurs, and an entirely different condition exists but is ignored and therefore not treated or corrected.
b. Behavioral problems of some children can be traced to teacher--pupil interactions, and the teacher may need to be corrected. Sole attention to the child's problem may lead to overlooking adjustments that the teacher may need to make.
c. The stereotype is correct, and the child receives the necessary treatment, providing it's available.

Another example involving children in the public schools is provided by Lambert, and others, in a study conducted in California. The authors found considerable variations in incidence of hyperkinesis based upon who does the case finding. When a strict medical diagnosis is used, less than 2 percent of school children are found to be hyperactive, whereas a school system count is over 12 percent.[71] Lambert's study is a prime example of the medicalization of deviance in which troublesome school children are transformed into pupils with medical disorders. They are labeled, perhaps separated from other pupils, and treated differently. Expectations by teachers for the child's performance in school may be lowered. Their treatment, by and large, is directed at achieving peace and tranquility in the schools. It is also an example of how medicalization promotes social control.

SELECTION OF DEVIANTS THROUGH STEREOTYPING

Stereotypes play a powerful role in those determinations and processes applicable to the initial selection of persons to whom deviant labels are to be applied. Persons who are responsible for dispensing labels use stereotypes to determine if the individual fits the category. In their study of police discretion, Irving Piliavin and Scott Briar show how a decision to charge two young men with the crime of statutory rape is based on the demeanor of the suspects. The youth who shows remorse regarding his behavior and respect for the police fares quite differently from the youth who does neither. The polite, remorseful youth is not "made" a delinquent while the sullen youth is.[72]

In selecting deviants for processing, the stereotypes held by the operative may play a more potent role than objective observation and analysis of the behavior in question. Whether this is due to prejudice or the pressures of the job or some combination of each is unknown. For example, reports of child abuse or neglect are generally received by the police or protective service worker (social worker) by telephone. An agent is then assigned to investigate this new referral in addition to maintaining responsibility for an existing high caseload. The agent typically has only sketchy, fragmented, and unsubstantiated information about the alleged abuse or neglect situation but does have a responsibility to ensure that the child is protected. Consequently, lack of information, constraints on the agent's time because of other pressing duties and various other job pressures combine to create a situation in which stereotyping becomes functional.

Other factors that influence the agent's decisions, while not directly related to the deviant act itself include the existence of a "record" of the individuals in the case, the amount and degree of remorse shown, and the alleged abuser's cooperation with the agent.

As noted earlier in this chapter there is a tendency to view deviance as an achieved status while racial and ethnic statuses are seen as ascribed. Attention to the mechanisms of stereotyping, however, suggest that individuals do not earn their way into deviant categories through their behavior; deviant categories are ascribed to them by others. In particular, these ascriptions are performed by label dispensers who exercise discretion in their decision making about whether or not to label. If, for illustration, we return to the example provided by Piliavin and Briar about two youths who are suspected of rape, only one becomes a deviant due to choices exercised by the police. These choices are not made on the basis of facts in the case, it is the facts that bring the youths to the attention of the police. The decision to label and process is based on the stereotypes police have about what a delinquent is like versus what a "good" boy is like. Decisions to create deviants through labeling are more closely related to stereotypes held by label dispensers than they are to the behavior of the rule violators.

A related example concerns the difficulties experienced by professionals in determining child abuse. Gross evidence of child abuse and accidental injury are frequently similar in appearance so that police officers, school teachers, and welfare workers must seek additional cues in making a determination of suspected abuse. Stereotypic images are gained as a result of journal articles on the subject, training programs, films and prior case experience and consist typically of parents who are poor, uneducated, perhaps unemployed, and generally unsophisticated. When people with these attributes appear with an injured child "the practitioner would seem likely to label that person an abuser." Someone who does not fit the stereotype may be more likely to avoid the label.[73]

There are reasons why we prefer to believe that the status of a deviant is an achieved one. It gives us comfort to think that there is a sharp and clear distinction between good and evil. We take comfort in knowing that other families are the bad ones and that they produce child abuse and delinquency. Stereotypes fuel this belief by providing a single, symbolic, and uncomplicated vision of the problem. This belief obscures the argument presented by labeling theorists, that the passageways to deviant careers begin with labeling and not behavior and that, for the most part, deviant statuses are ascribed and not achieved.

In this chapter, labels and stereotypes have been examined from the perspective of labeling theory, and some useful definitions have been presented. These concepts will be explored in more mundane and pragmatic contexts when they are examined in regard to how they are used by human service professionals and organizations.

REFERENCES

1. Erich Goode, *Deviant Behavior: An Interactionist Approach* (Englewood Cliffs, New Jersey: Prentice-Hall, Inc., 1978) p. 178.
2. Nicholas N. Kittrie, *The Right to be Different: Deviance and Enforced Therapy* (Baltimore: The Johns Hopkins Press, 1971) pp. 2–3.
3. Peter L. Berger and Thomas Luckmann, *The Social Construction of Reality* (Garden City, N.Y.: Doubleday, 1966).
4. Goode, *Deviant Behavior*, p. 11.
5. Peter Conrad and Joseph W. Schneider, *Deviance and Medicalization* (St. Louis, Missouri: The C. V. Mosby Company, 1980) p. 21.

6. Berger and Luckmann, *Social Construction*, p. 69.
7. Howard S. Becker, *Outsiders* (New York: The Free Press, 1963) p. 162.
8. Donald T. Dickson, "Bureaucracy and Morality: An Organizational Perspective on a Moral Crusade," *Social Problems, 16* (II, Fall): 143, 1963.
9. Eliot Freidson, *Profession of Medicine* (New York: Harper and Row, Publishers, Inc., 1970) p. 252.
10. Eliot Freidson, *Professional Dominance* (Chicago: Aldine Publishing Company 1970) p. 5.
11. Conrad and Schneider, *Medicalization*, pp. 269–270.
12. Janet B. W. Williams, "DSM–III: A Comprehensive Approach to Diagnosis." *Social Work*, 26 (II March): 101, 1981.
13. Thomas J. Scheff, "Cultural Stereotypes and Mental Illness," in *Deviance: The Interactionist Perspective*, eds. Earl Rubington and Martin S. Weinberg (Fourth ed.), (New York: MacMillan Publishing Co., Inc., 1978) p. 85.
14. Morris Janowitz, *The Last Half-Century: Societal Change and Politics in America* (Chicago: The University of Chicago Press, 1978) pp. 333–34.
15. Janowitz, *Last Half-Century*, pp. 341, 347.
16. M. J. McDermott and M. J. Hindelang, Analysis of National Crime Victimization Survey Data to Study Serious Delinquent Behavior, Monograph One—*Juvenile Criminal Behavior in the United States: Its Trends and Patterns* (Rockville, Maryland: Criminal Justice Research Center, 1981).
17. A. J. Rogers, III, *The Economics of Crime* (Hinsdale, Illinois: The Dryden Press, 1973) pp. 11–13.
18. Conrad and Schneider, *Deviance and Medicalization*, p. 226.
19. John Lofland, *Deviance and Identity* (Englewood Cliffs, N.J.: Prentice-Hall, Inc., 1969) p. 131.
20. *Family Weekly*, January 23, 1977.
21. Lofland, *Deviance and Identity*, p. 134.
22. Conrad and Schneider, *Deviance and Medicalization*, p. 69.
23. Richard J. Gelles, *Family Violence* (Beverly Hills, California: Sage Publications, Inc., 1979) p. 48.
24. David G. Gil, *Violence Against Children* (Cambridge, Mass.: Harvard University Press, 1970).
25. Edwin M. Lemert, *Social Pathology* (New York: McGraw-Hill Book Co., 1951) p. 75.
26. Edwin M. Lemert, *Human Deviance, Social Problems, and Social Control* (2nd Edition) (Englewood Cliffs, N.J.: Prentice-Hall, 1972) p. 42.
27. Joseph W. Eaton and Robert J. Weil, "The Mental Health of the Hutterites," in *Mental Illness and Social Processes*, ed. Thomas Scheff (New York: Harper and Row Publishers, 1967) pp. 92–101.
28. Eaton and Weil, "The Hutterites," p. 96.
29. Becker, *Outsiders*.
30. John I. Kitsuse and Raymond Dietrick, "Delinquent Boys: A Critique," *American Sociological Review, 24* (2):209–215, 1959.

31. Milton Mankoff, "Societal Reaction and Career Deviance: A Critical Analysis," *The Sociological Quarterly, 12* (Spring): 204–218, 1971.

32. Barry M. Dank, "Coming Out in the Gay World," *Psychiatry: Journal for the Study of Interpersonal Processes, 34:* 180–97, 1971.

33. Don C. Gibbons and Joseph F. Jones, *The Study of Deviance: Perspectives and Problems* (Englewood Cliffs, New Jersey: Prentice-Hall, Inc., 1975) p. 125.

34. Lemert, *Social Pathology,* p. 75.

35. Lemert, *Social Pathology,* p. 75.

36. Nanette J. Davis, *Sociological Constructions of Deviance* (Dubuque, Iowa: William C. Brown Company, 1975) p. 172.

37. Gibbons and Jones, *Study of Deviance,* p. 125.

38. Albert K. Cohen, "The Sociology of the Deviant Act: Anomie Theory and Beyond," *American Sociological Review,* 30 (February): 5–14, 1965.

39. Davis, *Sociological Construction,* p. 180.

40. Jonathan L. Freedman, David O. Sears, and J. Merrill Carlsmith, *Social Psychology* (3rd Edition) (Englewood Cliffs, New Jersey: Prentice-Hall, Inc., 1978) pp. 86–87.

41. Harold Sampson, Sheldon L. Messinger, and Robert D. Towne, "Family Processes and Becoming a Mental Patient," *The American Journal of Sociology, 68* (July): 88–96, 1962.

42. Charles H. McCaghy, *Deviant Behavior: Crime, Conflict and Interest Groups* (New York: MacMillan Publishing Co., Inc., 1976) p. 87.

43. Lemert, *Human Deviance,* p. 42.

44. Lemert, *Human Deviance,* p. 42.

45. Lemert, *Human Deviance,* p. 42.

46. Davis, *Sociological Construction,* p. 174.

47. Lemert, *Human Deviance,* p. 40.

48. Becker, *Outsiders.*

49. Erving Goffman, "The Moral Career of the Mental Patient," *Psychiatry: Journal for the Study of Interpersonal Processes, 22* (May): 123–135, 1959.

50. Robert A. Stebbins, *Commitment to Deviance* (Westport, Connecticut: Greenwood Publishing Corporation, 1971) p. 11

51. Cohen, "The Sociology of the Deviant Act," pp. 5–14.

52. Lemert, *Social Pathology,* pp. 77–78.

53. Davis, *Sociological Constructions,* p. 170.

54. Goode, *Deviant Behavior,* p. 179.

55. Goode, *Deviant Behavior,* p. 89.

56. Gordon W. Allport, *The Nature of Prejudice* (New York: Doubleday Anchor Books, 1958) p. 167.

57. Robert K. Merton, *Social Theory and Social Structure* (2nd edition) (New York: Free Press, 1957) p. 428.

58. Freedman, Sears, and Carlsmith, *Social Psychology,* p. 78.

59. J. L. Simmons, "Public Stereotypes of Deviants," in *The Substance of Sociology,*

ed. Ephraim H. Mizruchi (New York: Appleton-Century Crofts, 1967) pp. 271-282.

60. Edward Z. Dager, ed., *Socialization* (Chicago, Illinois: Markham Publishing Company, 1971) p. IX.

61. Edwin H. Sutherland, *White Collar Crime* (New York: Dryden, 1949).

62. Albert K. Cohen, *Deviance and Control* (Englewood Cliffs, New Jersey: Prentice-Hall, Inc., 1966) p. 30.

63. Simmons, "Public Stereotypes," p. 274.

64. Simmons, "Public Stereotypes," p. 279.

65. Ralph Hingson and others, *In Sickness and in Health* (St. Louis, Missouri: The C. V. Mosby Company, 1981) p. 19.

66. Conrad and Schneider, *Medicalization of Deviance.*

67. Conrad and Schneider, *Medicalization of Deviance,* p. 31.

68. Alex Kaplan, "The Conference on Improvements in Psychiatric Classification and Terminology (DSM-III)—A Report," *Newsletter of the American Psychoanalytic Association,* October 1976, 5.

69. Peter Schrag and Diane Divoky, *The Myth of the Hyperactive Child* (New York: Pantheon Books, Inc., 1975).

70. Jane R. Mercer, *Labeling the Mentally Retarded* (Berkeley, California: University of California Press, 1973) p. 7.

71. N. Lambert, V. Sandoval, and D. Sassone, "Prevalence of Hyperactivity in Elementary School Children as a Function of Social System Definers," *American Journal of Orthopsychiatry 48:* 446–443, 1978.

72. Irving Pilavin and Scott Briar, "Police Encounters with Juveniles," *American Journal of Sociology,* 70 (September): 206–214, 1964.

73. Gelles, *Family Violence,* p. 45.

Chapter 5

PROCESSES IN THE
DEVELOPMENT OF DEVIANT IDENTITIES

ALTERNATE RESPONSES TO SOCIAL REACTION

A number of facets of an important but poorly understood series of steps involved in the development of deviant identities will be explored in this chapter. In temporal terms, the discussion refers to that point following formal labeling where estimates have to be made, both by the discovered deviant and his or her handlers, as to what kind of person has done these things.

Consider, for example, the difference in the way the individual identifies self relative to a frame of reference in the following interchange: "Yes, I lied, but I am not a liar." The deviant behavior is admitted, but the deviant role of "liar" is denied. Now consider this statement: "I lied because I am a liar." The individual in presenting the latter statement has accomplished the transition from deviant act to deviant role. "I lied because I am a liar" may be a statement used as a defensive adaptation to being caught in a lie, a devil-may-care attitude, or even an effort to appear contrite. Regardless, the phrase identifies a personal recognition of an undesirable role. The transition from a normal to a deviant role as a consequence of processes involved in the social reaction to primary deviance is the subject of this chapter.

Much has been written about the rough processing given delinquents and adult offenders whereby they become alienated and subsequently plunged into the role of outcast that cements their sense of commitment to deviant values, perspectives, and careers. Far less attention has been devoted to those seemingly more benign interactive processes whereby many more innocent types of deviants find their former identities challenged and must grapple with a range of new or previously barely considered alternatives, none of which is entirely satisfactory.

In an early formulation of labeling theory, Edwin M. Lemert identifies a crucial interactional aspect involved in the evolution of deviant identities: "Deviations are not significant until they are organized subjectively and transformed into active roles and become the social criteria for assigning status. The deviant individuals must react symbolically to their own behavior aberrations and fix them in their socio-psychological patterns."[1]

The individual, in this view, must not only be aware of the nature of the social reaction to his or her deviant behavior but must also begin to internalize it before secondary deviance can be said to occur. The development of a deviant identity is not the outcome of a single episode, except in very rare instances, but occurs over time in a series of stages.[2] Within the temporal separation between primary and secondary deviance and even after the first signs of career deviance become evident, the individual usually has some opportunities to successfully deny to himself and others an identity as deviant. The extensive use of probation sentences by criminal court judges seem to take this conjecture into account. Although the individual has been apprehended, tried, convicted, and sentenced, his conforming life need not change substantially, and he need not adopt deviant response patterns. He may, with some success, continue to insist that "I lied, but I am not a liar." While circumstances vary and a record of conviction for a criminal offense can profoundly injure an individual's reputation, it is not sufficient in and of itself to push someone into a career in crime.

Life is full of examples of seriously disabled persons overcoming their disabilities or achieving worthwhile careers despite them. In an account of a well-publicized trial of a deaf-mute charged with murdering a prostitute, Ernest Tidyman describes the defense attorney, Lowell J. Myers, who is deaf:

> Deafness came upon him at a crucial stage of his development as a human being and instructed him cruelly in the daily humiliations of the severely handicapped. Profound hurt and helpless rage sometimes seized him. But he controlled it.
>
> Instead of seeking revenge and [finding] further humiliation, Myers turned the energy of his rage to the toughening process that bespeaks

survival. Highly intelligent and an excellent student, he enlarged and strengthened his talents as he used them in concentrated ways. He read and studied incessantly. He refused to allow his ambitions to be curtailed by his handicap, and instead tied them to the locomotion of aggressiveness. He learned lipreading and sign language and became highly skilled in both.

Lowell Myers became a Certified Public Accountant and, becoming bored with this profession, went on to law school and became an attorney, vowing to help the handicapped.[3]

Robert Merton's work concerning anomie poses a number of possible adaptations the individual may make to the social structure. Merton's typology of various adaptations to anomie can also be conceptualized in terms of the individual's response to the experience of being labeled. Thus the deviant may innovate by proclaiming himself or herself an ex-sinner, join, and take an active and highly visible role in a group dedicated to dietary or religious fundamentalism. Or, he or she may choose conformity and become a "paragon of virtue," ceasing not only deviant behavior but even the appearance of engaging in questionable activities such as drinking or smoking. Or, he or she may employ ritualistic or retreatist adaptations, move to another town, appear infrequently in public or become a "workaholic." The final adaptation proposed by Merton is rebellion, wherein the individual decides that he has been treated unfairly or sees no other avenue available to him, disregards conventional norms and pursues a deviant career.[4]

In considering Merton's proposed modes of adaptation to problems created by the social structure, it is evident that while social forces may impel people toward one or another type of adjustment the decision to continue engaging in deviant behavior involves a certain amount of personal choice by the individuals involved. Lemert deals specifically with this issue when he notes that:

> The importance of the person's conscious symbolic reactions to his or her own behavior cannot be overstressed in explaining the shift from normal to abnormal behavior.... This is not to say that conscious choice is a determining factor in the differentiating process [between normal and deviant roles].... But however it may be perceived, the individual's self-definition is closely connected with such things as self-acceptance, the subordination of minor to major roles, and with the

motivation involved in learning the skills, techniques, and values of a new role.[5]

Does this mean that some people knowingly and willingly pursue a career in deviance, that the deviant manufactures his own situation through conscious choice? To the extent that the penalties associated with claiming to be nondeviant are greater than the penalties associated with becoming a committed deviant, the individual exercises a more or less forced choice. It is a losing game, and the issue is how best to cut one's losses. As Thomas Scheff has observed, the mental patient who continues to deny that he is insane may escape self-definition as a deviant, but is nevertheless punished or denied certain limited rewards for not playing the stereotyped deviant role. "Thus the ex-mental patient, although he is urged to rehabilitate himself in the community, usually finds himself discriminated against in seeking to return to his old status, and on trying to find a new one in the occupational, marital, social, and other spheres."[6]

The nature of personal choices pursued by the individual are, in addition, limited by available social roles, opportunities, and the expectations of others. For example, an elderly employee may decide to retire and expect to fill his or her time with various leisure pursuits, a hobby or two, some community service activity, and lots of visiting with out-of-state relatives. Should these opportunities be nonexistent, or erode over time, the elderly individual will find that his or her prior affiliations with work and recreational groups have probably been lost and that the reorganization of one's identity around the position of the retired is most unsatisfactory. As Zelma Smith Blau has pointed out, one of the ironies of old age is that when an individual needs substitute roles most, alternatives become less available than had been the norm earlier in life.[7] The available deviant role is one of withdrawal and isolation from the community, disengagement from productive tasks, and a generalized withering of existing skills and intellectual capabilities from underutilization.

COMMITMENT TO DEVIANCE

The term *commitment* as used here refers to a forced choice arrangement, that is, the individual must choose between two or more courses, but the choice is his or hers. Individuals become committed to a line of conduct or an identity because of "their awareness of the impossibility of choosing a different social identity or rejecting a particular expectation because of the imminence of penalties involved."[8] Penalties may refer to actual infliction of pain or to the restriction of movement as when a deviant is removed to an institution; but the element of choice is virtually non-existent in this example. It is those penalties that affect one emotionally or psychologically, that assault one's self-image, and force a choice that commits the individual to a deviant career that are of concern here. These are problems of ideology, of how one looks at the world and justifies one's behavior in it while maintaining an acceptable self-image.

Let us take the case of a woman who is a heavy drinker. Over an extended period she receives a number of traffic citations for drunk driving. She has been labeled, and a record of her offenses exists. Her deviance is formally recognized. Does she think, "I am a worthless person and a bad mother because I drink too much?" Her perception of the label and the social reaction may take any one of three forms, namely, "I am not an alcoholic, like any other person there are lapses in my behavior; or I can escape the legal consequences of the label and find an excuse for my behavior by beginning psychiatric treatment; or I can accept the label alcoholic and enter Alcoholics Anonymous or some other treatment program for those like me."

If she chooses the first option, denial, she may be able to preserve a positive self-image for a time, but she is likely to receive the harshest legal penalties. The second option offers a form of partial denial since she can claim to be suffering from emotional problems and not alcoholism. Her positive self-image, while partially eroded by a mental illness label, can remain somewhat intact since she can rationalize to herself that everyone has emotional problems at one time or another. If she selects the final option, acceptance of the label alcoholic, she is apt to receive the most negative sanctions from her friends, more distant family members, and neighbors and, in turn, feel really rotten about herself. She will be an alcoholic in a society that holds persons responsible for behavior that they presumably can control, and the woman may enter a treatment program, like Alcoholics Anonymous, that routinely reminds her of who and what she is.

Commitment, then, is a process characterized in its initial stages by calculations that deviants engage in concerning penalties, risks, and losses. Julius Roth, in an important book dealing with the adjustment of tuberculosis patients to their treatment states the case clearly in relation to time and time estimates which the patients feel they need to know but which are not provided by the medical staff. The patient doesn't want to be in the hospital but is aware that he may die if he or she doesn't submit to treatment.

> The first impression one gets of the TB patient's concern with time is that everyone is frantically trying to find out how long he is in for. The new patient questions the doctors, nurses, and other hospital personnel in an effort to discover how many years, months, and days it will take him to be cured. . . . He compares his case with those of his ward mates, other patients who visit the ward, patients who have left the hospital (about whom stories are told by the remaining patients) in an effort to find which of them has a condition and treatment regimen that most closely approximates his own, and therefore, about what time in the future he can expect given phases of treatment and discharge from the hospital.[9]

Most patients who enter the hospital, in Roth's study, thought that they had mild cases of tuberculosis and would recover soon. They discover after awhile that this is not the case, and they press for a timetable, meanwhile becoming submerged in a subculture of deprived but struggling people.

These calculations that deviants enter into are certainly not well-developed cost-benefit analyses nor are they invariably entirely conscious estimates of the options available in any threatening situation. They are more like a gambler's choice that good luck, above all else, will hopefully determine the outcome.

INTERACTIONS OF PROFESSIONALS AND DEVIANTS

An oft-repeated statement provided by the human service professional in the early stages of treatment is that "it takes strength to seek help." While this statement has been undoubtedly engendered to counteract the American ethic of standing on one's own two feet and thereby not seeking help for one's problems, it cuts to a deeper truth when we consider the meaning of commitment. Once the individuals seek help or agree to receive it, their ability to deny that they are that sort of (deviant) person is sharply reduced. By remaining in therapy the individual admits, however tentatively, that he or she and not others, is the problem.

The decision by the individual to obtain help is frequently surmised to be a positive step toward normalcy or at least an effort by the person to cease or interrupt a deviant career. Yet, as in the example of the woman who enters therapy because of a drinking problem, it is also the confirmation of a deviant identity. Neighbors, friends, and relatives appear to be less rejecting of an individual who displays deviant behavior than they are of the same person who has their deviant status confirmed by seeking treatment.

In an important study of rejection, based upon the help source utilized, Derek L. Phillips interviewed 300 respondents in a southern New England town. Case abstracts of four mentally ill and one normal person were presented in combination with information about what help source the individuals were utilizing. Phillips hypothesis that "individuals exhibiting identical behavior will be increasingly rejected as they are described as not seeking any help, as using a clergyman, a physician, a psychiatrist, or a mental hospital," was proven correct. The largest increase in rejection occurs when the individual is described as consulting a psychiatrist. Those help sources that can be identified as specific to mental illness receive disproportionate rejection scores.[10] Other studies have indicated similar findings wherein people tend to have strong negative attitudes towards psychiatrists and mental hospitals as well as toward individuals using them.* There is no reason to believe that the individual seeking help is unaware of the likelihood of rejection or that these feelings are not shared by the person in the form of self-rejection.

*See, for example, Elaine and John Cumming, *Closed Ranks: An Experiment in Mental Health Education* (Cambridge: Harvard University Press, 1957); Judith Rabkin, "Public Attitudes toward Mental Illness: A Review of the Literature," *Schizophrenia Bulletin, 10*(Fall):9–33, 1974.

The forced choice of the labeled individual actually involves two entirely different forms of commitment, one conforming, the other nonconforming. The nonconforming choice is to continue to engage in deviant behavior while disregarding, ignoring, or relegating to minor significance the reactions of others. The individual may find it necessary to rearrange their values in order to reduce self-rejection and, in turn, reject those who are doing the rejecting. Or, the individuals may select the conforming choice and commit themselves to the deviant role of being in treatment with a human service professional.

EXAMPLES OF TWO TYPES OF DEVIANT ROLES

Nonconforming role	*Conforming role*
heavy drinker, drunkard	alcoholic
disturbed person, crazy	mental patient, mentally ill
malperforming public school pupil	retarded, emotionally impaired, etc.

Both conforming and nonconforming deviant roles possess a number of similarities although we are accustomed to thinking about them as being very different. Both sets of roles are responded to negatively by social audiences and are frequently stereotyped by observers. These social responses mark the individual, whether fulfilling a conforming or nonconforming deviant role, as a disvalued person. On the other hand, judgements about the actor in the nonconforming role are made largely on the basis of observed behavior while audiences evaluate the actor playing the conforming role in respect to a label that has been ascribed. The label alone is sufficient evidence that the actor is deviant. Another difference between the two includes the likelihood that nonconforming roles fail to assume the proportions of master statuses and therefore such individuals are not defined as deviant by all audiences and are rarely defined as being deviant all the time by close friends, relatives and fellow employees. Conforming role behavior, such as engaging in treatment, may at times meet with considerable approval by intimate audiences, such as the individual's family or close friends, or perhaps by an interested school teacher or supervisor who knew the actor prior to the onset of the deviant behavior. This approval, however, is likely to be contingent upon visible behavioral signs of successful treatment and tends to drop off precipitously when deviant behavior noted earlier recurs.

PROCESSES IN THE DEVELOPMENT OF DEVIANT CAREERS

If conforming role commitment is chosen, the individual is likely to encounter a number of processes that fully immerses her or him in an unfamiliar but deviant role, that of client or patient. The client may voluntarily seek help or may do so under duress, but in any event he or she is about to encounter an agency and its professional staff. The client is new to this situation, unless he or she has been down this path before, while the professional staff are not only accustomed to such a client but view his or her entry as part of their routine. The processes that I wish to examine have been put forward by Edwin M. Schur and include stereotyping, retrospective interpretation, negotiation, and role engulfment.[11] They arise from both professional and bureaucratic sources and vary by organizational mandate and type of clientele.

Stereotyping

In Chapter 4, a discussion on the ways in which stereotypes affect our thoughts about deviants was largely confined to public stereotyping and the increasing medicalization of deviance. Stereotyping, however, is not only a public phenomenon that results in distorted information about deviance and the behavior of deviants. It is also a mechanism used in the creation of conforming or treated deviants by human service organizations and professionals.

The new role formulated for the deviant, that of patient or client, engages the actor in a set of new, interactive obligations or requirements with the treatment organization and its agents. The client must assume or give the impression of assuming that the professional knows what is best for him or her and must actively participate in the prescribed therapy. To fail to cooperate is a sign that the client has fallen back into his or her former deviant ways or has never really abandoned them. The role that the professional expects the client to fill is fashioned out of stereotypical images of what "good" clients are like. Indeed, this type of stereotyping may be based upon the experience professionals have had with successful cases where the deviance has been less pronounced or of a lesser magnitude. Clients who cooperate with professionals, appear on time for interviews, and are able to articulate their feelings may do better than those who do not. Those clients who are dealing with their own deviant identities are particularly sensitive to the perceptions that professionals have about them. Above all, they may wish to appear as being good persons despite the problems they face. They sense that a positive judgement by the professional is important to their fate. They soon learn that if they accept the proferred deviant identity even though they may feel that it doesn't truly represent them, they will be seen as being cooperative.

Both public and professional stereotypes are useful in reducing the need to engage in complex assessments of those with whom we come into contact. In this sense they are functional. Public stereotypes, however, are founded on imagery that may have little or no basis in fact. Walter R. Gove suggests that a phenomenon of our culture is a stereotype of mental illness, perpetuated by the media, that presents such severe and bizarre behavior that most real persons and families do not recognize that they may have a mental illness. This is true, even if these persons are actively engaged in treatment, because their own symptoms do not seem to fit the stereotype.[12] Public stereotypes also serve to convince people that they have much to fear from deviants.

Professional stereotypes, on the other hand, are generalizations about kinds of people that have some basis in data, such as demographics, research findings, or experience. For example personnel who fill roles in hospital emergency units must be able to deal quickly and efficiently with incoming patients and differentiate between cases based upon seemingly superficial appearances. They draw upon professional stereotypes in making preliminary diagnostic judgements to accomplish these decisions. By the same token a student of mine might visit the university's health service offices complaining of chest pains. The physician on duty may very well ask him what kind of pizza he had for lunch. However, if a portly, aging faculty member entered the same complaint the physician is likely to suspect a heart attack. "Diagnostic categories

are stereotypes in the sense that they identify a cluster of characteristics typically associated with various disorders."[13]

In professional education the presentation and analysis of cases
and conditions is a form of stereotyping. *Depression* is not only a
textbook term followed by a listing of associated symptomology, it
is also a condition that affects real people who are described
graphically in classroom lectures and readings. In professional
education these stereotypes are constructed through the building
of inferential generalizations about classes of phenomena so that
coherent images emerge that are later recognized and remembered
by the student. This training is intended to encourage students to
organize their thinking around verifiable scientific generalizations,
reduce prejudging of behavior based on personal moral standards,
and have them question the applicability of a particular stereotype to the case in question. Therefore, labels in this context are
both a product of the act of stereotyping as well as a set of formal
stereotypes.

The extent to which these objectives are achieved is the subject
of an exploratory study conducted by Lois P. Case and Neverlyn
B. Lingerfelt. In their study concerning stereotyping by social
workers the authors examined "the question of whether the degree
of labeling increases with the educational level of the labeler."
They found that "labeling increases with the amount of professional education."[14] Our understanding of professional stereotyping suggests that this effect is precisely what is intended; the
supplanting of old, superficial, and moralistic notions about people
with new, more precise, and functional categories. In addition,
professional education attempts to reduce judgementalism in its
students by training them to evaluate others objectively. Therefore,
professionally trained and experienced social workers should be
more likely to categorize people in a systematic and objective
fashion.

The researchers found, however, that, in addition to a greater
frequency of labeling, the use of negative adjectives and nouns
increased with the extent of education and experience of the
respondents. The more highly trained and experienced social
workers not only used such words as paranoid and depressive
more frequently than the less trained groups but also referred to

subjects with words like uncooperative and sullen. Case and Lingerfelt summarize their study by noting that "as the student acquires professional distance he also learns to be selectively attentive to the negative aspects of the client's personality. This transition is accentuated when the student becomes affiliated with a social service agency."[15]

While more research is needed on issues such as this, some tentative observations can be offered. First, public stereotypes tend to endure and, to an extent, become reified within human service organizations. Professional training in the use of functional stereotypes is problematic because of the negative aura of these categories. The negative affect that accompanies professional stereotyping appears to be even further extended when they are put to use in human service organizations. Second, clients, upon entering treatment, have considerable concern about the depth and extent of their deviant identity. To a greater or lesser extent, they share in the feelings of others toward them and their labels. Since, to a certain degree, almost all people in our culture are socialized similarly in reference to images of deviants, the client tends to have the same beliefs, attitudes, and values about social identity that the public does. Clients will therefore be subject to hold the same convictions that others hold about stereotypes. Soon after entering treatment they may find that although professionals mask their true feelings, they tend to hold perspectives about clients that resemble public stereotypes. As a consequence, clients will feel, at least early in the treatment encounter, that they are becoming unmasked as being true deviants. Many will attempt to evade these feelings and attitudes towards themselves by dropping out of treatment.

Retrospective Interpretation

Should the individual continue to participate in treatment, he or she will be faced with another process that may serve to confirm a deviant identity, that of retrospective interpretation. Schur describes this as a mechanism by which reactors come to view deviators or suspected deviants "in a totally new light." He notes that "one of the most intriguing and systematic forms of retrospective interpretation of deviance occurs in the organizational processing of deviators and involves the use of the 'case history.' "[16]

In Chapter 2, the significance of the client's biography in developing an understanding of the origins of the deviance in certain psychological approaches was discussed. Retrospective interpretation is a process used in treatment situations to gather biographical material from clients that is then reinterpreted relative to their current state or condition. The professional poses questions aimed at eliciting from the client an explanation for his or her present circumstances. The professional, instead of equally emphasizing information relevant to both positive and negative aspects of the client's life, tends to focus mainly on the negative content. This content is then linked to an earlier, unpleasant life event or pattern. Much of the material that is elicited is denigrating; positive feelings and events in the client's past receive scant attention. Material related to conflict, childhood trauma, early sexual experimentation, and sibling rivalry is brought to the foreground, and a new salience is given to it in light of more recent troubling and negative events. The client is led to believe that what he or she is now has been so all along. It is in this way that the deviant identity is confirmed.

For persons who are suspected of engaging in child abuse, retrospective interpretation can be a process that connects a current diagnostic guess with a history of past deviance. Although the information that is connected may be true, it is the attempt to discover patterns of abuse that is potentially most damaging. As children, many parents were beaten on occasion or even regularly by their parents. Many children have an alcoholic parent or an unemployed father. Extreme tensions provoke sporadic violence in many families. Taken separately, these are unfortunate but not abnormal occurrences in people's lives. Viewed through the process of retrospective interpretation, these incidents constitute a history of factors likely to contribute to child abuse.

An interesting version of retrospective interpretation is the generational model in which the "sins" of the parents are revisited by the children later in life. Srinika Jayaratne defines the model as

The generational phenomenon of child abuse is one of the most commonly held conceptions (or misconceptions) about abusing parents. The essence of this proposition is that the victim of abuse incorporates patterns of aggression, which are then repeated from generation to generation. This position is illustrated in the works of numerous authors. . . . Despite the formidable array of authors and studies, Kadushin, in reviewing the literature, concluded: "There is little valid evidence to support the theory that abusive parents were themselves abused as children." . . . With regard to the generational hypothesis of child abuse, the author is somewhat skeptical.[17]

Despite a lack of empirical support for the generational model, its adaptation to professional practice is smooth and comfortable. The model offers an opportunity for a level of justification and satisfaction on the part of both the professional and the client. For the professional it becomes useful as a diagnostic cue and a form of evidence that recent abuse has probably occurred. For the client, it is perceived as an ameliorating factor; the guilt for having engaged in abusive behavior is reduced since it is not entirely his or her fault. Blame rests with the historical parent, the parent's parents. It is in this way that the generational model is truly seductive, and retrospective interpretation becomes a process that "proves itself."

Prior to the process of retrospective interpretation, it was possible for the individual to personally separate himself or herself from the deviant behavior, to view it as not part of one's essential self. Indeed, clients will say, "I entered therapy to find out why I do those awful things." The meaning of this statement is that those "awful things" stand in opposition to the basically "good person that I really am." The process of retrospective interpretation proves otherwise by revealing the deviance as a longstanding and enduring pattern and not an incidental one. What the person is now was there all along.

The individual who has his or her character assaulted through the processes of stereotyping and retrospective interpretation is not without personal resources and may call upon these in order to maintain some vestige of positive self-image. We should note, however, that it is a losing game, and the individual is usually willing to settle for an identity "that is not as bad as it looks." To accomplish this need for a strategy for preserving some part of a ruined character, the client must negotiate with the human service professional.

Negotiation

The clearest example of negotiation is in "plea bargaining," a type of interaction wherein the accused offender enters into an agreement with the prosecutor to plead guilty to a lesser charge in return for the promise of a more lenient sentence. This example parallels other deviants' more oblique negotiations for a lighter or less severe deviant label. Women, for example, are likely to avoid seeking treatment for alcoholism at agencies and programs specifically established for this purpose because the label is such a devastating one. They will, instead, attempt to receive treatment from family physicians or community-based mental health facilities. Once in treatment they will report that their problems have resulted from serious situational and emotional factors, such as desertion by the husband, illness, death of a family member, or unemployment. If they are successful in negotiating a label other than alcoholism, they may be able to avoid the stronger stigma attached to being an alcoholic.

Negotiation is a much more common process than most of us realize. The tuberculosis or cancer patient, among others, may refuse to accept an initial diagnosis which offers no hope. Typically, the professional literature refers to this as "denial," which, indeed, may be an accurate description of the patient's motivation. As a process, however, negotiation can be seen as an interactive phenomenon that, like plea bargaining, reduces the severity of the "sentence." It can be viewed as a strength rather than a weakness since negotiation represents an effort on the part of the client to maintain some element of normalcy in the face of a master status which offers little or no hope at all.

There are two particularly interesting facets to negotiation that are directly related to the development of career deviance in the person. One is that negotiation is a learned skill. Those who deviate and are caught at it learn to utilize techniques that serve to mitigate the effects of sanctions and frequently become skilled in ways of manipulating human service professionals. They may even learn which of the agencies in the community are most likely to give them what they want and, perhaps, which professionals are most pliable. The development of such skills are common features in all manner of career pursuits, both conforming and deviant ones. The college student, for example, soon learns which professors require the most exacting work and offer the lowest grades.

A second facet of negotiation is that participants implicitly recognize and learn to deal with power relationships. People who negotiate do so from relative positions of strength. If one side has none, there is no reason for the other side to negotiate. Why should the psychiatrist be willing to negotiate with his or her patient when typically the power differential is clear and uncontested? For one thing, the patient is capable of withholding cooperation, which could force the psychiatrist into a defending or cajoling role. Psychiatrists, physicians, and other human service professionals do their best work when the patient or client plays the role expected of them. The roles of the helper and client are complementary and, to an extent, one controls the other. To gain the patient's compliance, the psychiatrist will usually find it necessary to negotiate. Second, in many situations, the patient may be able to withdraw from the relationship entirely. Dyadic relationships, by definition, are terminated when one or another actor withdraws. If the relationship is not rewarding or fails to present the promise of future rewards, it is likely to be abandoned by one or both actors. Rewards in dyadic relationships are negotiable.

Included in the items the client may seek to negotiate are the frequency of treatment sessions, the content of reports to authorities such as the court, the extent of confidentiality afforded, and, most importantly, the diagnosis or label. Once clients realize that it is their own newly discovered negotiating skills that have brought them victories in these areas, they are well on their way to deviant role engulfment.

Role Engulfment

According to Schur, the final process in establishing career deviance is "the tendency of the deviator to become 'caught up in' a deviant role, to find that it has become salient in his overall personal identity (or concept of self), that his behavior is increasingly organized 'around' the role, and that cultural expectations attached to the role have come to have precedence, or increased salience relative to other expectations, in the organization of his activities and general way of life."[18]

The centrality of the deviant role, then, conditions all other roles in the individual's life and influences all interpersonal relations. Others are regarded as safe, neutral, to be avoided, or feared by the deviant individual based upon a calculation of where they stand relative to the individual's deviant identity. Individuals may join deviant subcultures, gangs, and the like, which consist of a body of shared solutions to the problems created in trying to manage a deviant identity.

While the process of role engulfment has been explored frequently in the deviance literature in relationship to criminals, prostitutes, and illicit drug users and their deepening commitment to these roles, the concept applies equally well to the careers of others who enter into treatment with human service professionals. For example, persons with physical disabilities and handicaps are treated with a special medical tolerance. Like the victim of acute illness, the handicapped person is excused from ordinary role obligations and is expected to conform to the sick role. The person is not held responsible for the condition but is expected to actively cooperate with rehabilitation personnel and closely follow the prescribed treatment regimen. The person's rights of self-assertion, independence, privacy, and dignity are subordinated to following instructions and engaging in behaviors that are prescribed for "getting well." They move into a fully dependent role, learn their limitations, and, it is hoped, eventually achieve as much mobility and freedom as their condition allows. Along the way they are engulfed by the sick role. Should the professional define the disabled person exclusively in terms of his or her handicap it is likely that these demoralizing interactions will result in a pattern of learned inferiority.

Degrading conceptions of the client can be embedded in even the most mundane actions of staff in human service organizations. At times, clients become particularly sensitive to these conceptions and may attempt to resist role engulfment with dire consequences, as in the following example: A young adult male resident of a group home for the mentally retarded approaches a staff member requesting some aspirin. Even though the resident may purchase aspirin on his own through nearby stores he was required to comply with the rigid rules surrounding this minor event. The staff member inquired as to why the aspirin was needed which is part of the routine procedure for dispensing nonprescriptive medication within the group home. At this, the resident began to pound his head with his fist, shouting "I can't do a damn thing around here without someone questioning me. I've got a headache. What do you think?" The resident then went to his room where he broke out all the windows.

Contingencies abound, however, in regard to the precipitators and accelerators of role engulfment. In the natural environment people may seek to immerse themselves more fully into deviant roles due to the gratification it brings or the problems it solves. Certain gamblers, heavy drinkers, and delinquents may opt for role engulfment as a relatively free choice. Others, finding themselves in treatment situations, have fewer choices but still manage to exercise a modicum of self-determination. Erving Goffman's discussion of the "moral career" of the mental patient identifies how institutionalized individuals perceive and respond to their treatment, eventually orienting themselves to the "ward system" and acceptance of the sick role.[19] The sick role, however, is not a single entity nor is it static. Patients seek to determine how well or how poorly they are doing relative to subtle "benchmarks" in the treatment situation and attempt to negotiate better prognoses with their keepers.[20] Imprisoned deviants, for example, may become "cons," enter deeply into the prison subculture or, conversely, remain aloof from it while preserving normative attitudes and values.

The human service professional is faced with a cruel dilemma in seeking to entice, cajole, or pressure the individual into client role engulfment. By requiring the individual to admit what he or she is in order to gain the client's cooperation in the treatment regimen, the professional insists that the client squarely face his or her behavior or condition. The heavy drinker must acknowledge that he or she is an alcoholic and will always be one. The

being a drunkard can be a self-handicapping strategy so failure can be blamed on the drinking not on ones innate character paraplegic must recognize that neither sensation nor movement will return to the lower half of his or her body. Such acknowledgements and recognitions take the form of confessions that demonstrate that the individual has accepted the "proof" of their deviant identity. They also reflect the fact that the professional is causing the client pain by insisting on these admissions. Hope, too, is offered, but it is entirely contingent upon the individual entering client role engulfment.

In summarizing this chapter it can be concluded that choices exist for most labeled deviants who come to the attention of human service professionals. For many, there are three choices available. Continued denial of the validity of the label to one's self and others is one possibility. Becoming committed to deviance is another. The third possibility, becoming a client or patient, is an equally perilous route, a consideration not often appreciated by human service professionals. The latter two courses have a common feature in that they involve the individual in admitting to a deviant identity.

REFERENCES

1. Edwin M. Lemert, *Social Pathology* (New York: McGraw-Hill Book Co., 1951) p. 75.
2. Albert K. Cohen, *Deviance and Control* (Englewood Cliffs, New Jersey: Prentice-Hall, Inc., 1966) p. 44.
3. Ernest Tidyman, *Dummy* (Boston, Mass.: Little, Brown and Company, Bantam Edition, 1975) pp. 21–22.
4. Robert K. Merton, *Social Theory and Social Structure* (Glencoe: The Free Press, 1962) p. 140.
5. Lemert, *Social Pathology,* p. 74.
6. Thomas J. Scheff, "Cultural Stereotypes and Mental Illness," in *Deviance: The Interactionist Perspective* (4th ed.), eds. Earl Rubington and Martin S. Weinberg (New York: Macmillan Publishing Co., Inc., 1981) p. 87.
7. Zelma Smith Blau, *Old Age in a Changing Society* (New York: New Viewpoints, 1973) p. 42.
8. Robert Stebbins, *Commitment to Deviance: The Non-Professional Criminal in the Community* (Westport, Connecticut: Greenwood Publishing Corporation, 1971) p. 35
9. Julius A. Roth, *Timetables* (Indianapolis: The Bobbs-Merrill Company, Inc. 1963) xvi–xvii.

10. Derek L. Phillips, "Rejection: A Possible Consequence of Seeking Help for Mental Disorders," in *Deviant Behavior: Readings in the Sociology of Deviance*, ed. Delos H. Kelly (New York: St. Martin's Press, 1979) pp. 425–439.

11. Edwin M. Schur, *Labeling Deviant Behavior: Its Sociological Implications* (New York: Harper and Row, Publishers, 1971).

12. Walter R. Gove, *The Labeling of Deviance* (Beverly Hills: Sage Publications, 1980) p. 103.

13. Nancy Atwood, "Professional Prejudice and the Psychotic Client," *Social Work, 27(2)* (March): 173, 1982.

14. Lois P. Case and Neverlyn B. Lingerfelt, "Name Calling: The Labeling Process in the Social Work Interview," *Social Service Review, 48(1)* (March): 76, 1974.

15. Case and Lingerfelt, "Name Calling," p. 83.

16. Schur, *Labeling Deviant Behavior,* p. 53.

17. Srinika Jayaratne, "Child Abusers As Parents and Children: A Review," Social Work, *22(1)* (January): 7. 1977.

18. Schur, *Labeling Deviant Behavior,* p. 69.

19. Erving Goffman, "The Moral Career of the Mental Patient," *Psychiatry, 22* (May): 123–135, 1959.

20. Roth, *Timetables.*

Chapter 6

PROFESSIONALS,
ORGANIZATIONS, AND DEVIANCE

SOCIAL CONTROL

Many deviance theorists depict the labeling process as "resulting characteristically in the reinforcement and crystallization of deviant behavior as a life style. This negative result is attributed to what are considered to be typical sequelae of the labeling process, namely, the isolation of the deviant from nondeviant social relationships and a resultant acceptance of a definition of self as a deviant person."[1] Considerably less attention has been drawn to those circumstances and situations in which labeling reduces or forestalls further deviant activity on the part of the individual and serves to reintegrate the person back into his or her primary group. Consideration of those circumstances that can yield positive effects from labeling will be discussed in the final chapter. This chapter continues our examination of labeling as an interactive process and presents a shift in focus from the reactions of the deviant to the actions of the labelers.

A brief review of the meaning of the concept social control may help to put this chapter into perspective. A considerable portion of the literature on deviance examines the deliberate effects of society's efforts to control those who deviate. Social control is transacted by the police, the courts, probation officers, prison guards, and attendants in mental hospitals as sanctions calculated to produce conformity in deviants. In the process deviators are said to be dehumanized. The view presented is actually one of coercive control wherein machinery is set in motion to force compliance by the deviator. Compliance is to be achieved by negative sanctions and punishments in place of the more normative means available to realize control, such as interpersonal

118

influence. It should be noted, however, that all societies, actually, all human aggregates, establish preferred patterns of conduct for social interaction, for task achievement, and for preserving the group. These preferred patterns of conduct become norms against which the behavior of people are evaluated.

For a variety of reasons, some individuals depart from or do not live up to these normative standards and meet with group disapproval. This pattern occurs not only in formal society but also in informal associations and subcultures. As Arthur Lewis Wood observes, "We can assert . . . that the use of mores and folkway as the bases for evaluating behavior is not simply a middleclass manifestation of capitalistic societies. There is no evidence for thinking that it is possible for society to rid itself of the fundamental social processes of norm formation and their essential character as standards for evaluating behavior."[2]

Morris Janowitz, tracing the intellectual history of the concept of social control by exploring the topic of societal change in the United States, decries the current usage that equates social control with coercion. He notes, "The opposite of social control can be thought of as coercive control, that is, the social organization of a society which rests predominantly and essentially on the use of force." Instead, social control can be conceived of as "a perspective that focuses on the capacity of a social organization to regulate itself" and therefore, "to the extent that it is effective, motivates social groups."[3] This is not to imply that the implementation of social control does not involve the use of power; but, if the power mode utilized is force, we can surmise that social control has failed.

The definition of social control provided by Wood is more specific to deviant behavior than that of Janowitz. He states that social control is "The use of power with the intention of influencing the behavior of others."[4] Both definitions, while being posed at different levels of abstraction, utilize key words that possess a degree of similarity, that is, *motivates* and *influences*. These are words that pertain to the intentions of human service professionals to which we will turn shortly.

Amitai Etzioni, in analyzing power in organizations, offers three subtypes of power which differ according to the means employed to make the subjects comply:

1. *Coercive power,* which "rests on the application, or the threat of application of physical sanctions, . . . restriction of movement; or controlling through force the satisfaction of needs such as those for food, sex, [and] comfort. . . . "
2. "*Remunerative power,* which is based on control over material resources and rewards. . . . "
3. *Normative power,* which "rests on the allocation and manipulation of symbolic rewards and deprivations: including influence over the distribution of acceptance and positive response and manipulation of esteem, prestige, and valued symbols such as awards."[5]

As noted earlier deviance theorists have tended to focus their concerns on the application of coercive power to control deviants. Coercion may produce immediate results in the desired direction, but is highly transitory and ultimately tends to produce alienation in the subject. Human service professionals are aware of this and tend not to use coercion in their work or to use it only as a last resort. Organizations that employ human service professionals, however, such as mental hospitals, prisons, and juvenile training schools may routinely empower nonprofessional staff to apply coercive measures to gain control. Restriction of movement tends to be a favored means of control. The nature of involvement of clients typically takes on the characteristics of apathetic conformity interspersed with sporadic resistance.

Remunerative power, as described by Etzioni, typically refers to employer–employee relationships that have as their basis salaries and wages and other material means of reward or recompense.[6] The discussion of negotiation in the last chapter makes it apparent that remunerative power can be applied to client–professional interactions as well. While the pay-off may not be in materials, clients who successfully negotiate for less time in treatment, an early release, a change to another ward in a mental hospital, or a favorable report from a therapist to a judge recognize that what they are after is quite tangible.

A more direct and practitioner-controlled use of remunerative power can be found in the practice of behavior modification, especially in the form of the "token economy" where specific rewards are offered to the client for behavioral compliance.[7] It is important to note that the "token economy" has appeared in settings such as juvenile correctional programs, institutions for the retarded, and residential facilities for disturbed children, among others, which formerly relied on coercion to achieve compliance. Janowitz takes a positive view of this development in noting that "behavior modification . . . has emerged as an intellectually based strategy with explicit linkages to the university-trained professionals" and that it represents "positive contributions to the search for social control and the reduction of interpersonal coercion."[8]

The third means of producing compliance posed by Etzioni is the use of normative power. He suggests that "a more eloquent name for this power would be persuasive, or manipulative, or suggestive power" but prefers not to use these terms since they have negative value connotations.[9] Leaving this caution aside, we propose that these terms are well-suited to fit the exercise of power most preferred by human service professionals who have a primary interest in the humane management of interpersonal relations. Their intent, by and large, is to gain compliance through the social psychological process known as persuasion, which Talcott Parsons defines as the use of symbolic means of communication in an attempt to effect a modification in the orientation, attitudes, or intentions of a person without changing the objective situation of rewards and punishments for action.[10]

The use of persuasion by the human service professional is intended to produce "moral involvement" on the part of the client whereby compliance is achieved through internalization of norms and, perhaps identification with the professional.[11] Furthermore, the professional attempts, through persuasion, to convince the client that all desired changes in behavior are in the client's best interests. Influencing the client and instilling motivation to change, rather than coercion, are generally the goals of the human service professional.

What, then, are the impediments to a realization of effective social control? If the human service professional is truly interested in achieving a reduction of pain and discomfort in the client and in uniting well-being with societal betterment, why the difficulty? Why should clients be at times timid and at other times recalcitrant about accepting a label designation as a necessary precursor to individual change? On the other hand, why is the state of the art of dispensing accurate labels so poor? Why is there so little agreement among professionals about the accuracy of label designations in specific cases and a recognized lack of unanimity in the human service field about the intrinsic value of any one classification system?

In my opinion the entire arena of labeling has been mystified, primarily by professionals, so that labels tend to serve as barriers to effective treatment and are distrusted by both clients and professionals. The use of such terms as neurotic tendencies, oral personality, and anal retentive configuration as well as psychopath and sociopath are symptomatic of a field in disarray and in need of demystification. A label is nothing more than a convenient identification of a state or condition that is to be corrected. It has no value in itself except insofar as the state can be corrected or eliminated. When this is achieved, relabeling can then occur.

RELABELING ASSUMPTIONS

Labeling theory poses a cruel dilemma for the responsible human service professional. If labeling and the concomitant processes of stereotyping, retrospective interpretation, negotiation, and role engulfment tend to produce career deviance, then what is the point of intervening at all? For one thing, all the facts are not in. The particular elements of the counseling relationship that are crucial to providing effective help have only recently come under serious study.[12] For another, labeling cannot simply be discarded because it is known that certain forms of deviance such as alcoholism cause tremendous problems for the individuals involved that will continue or get worse if the condition is unrecognized. The experience of alcoholic women who negotiate for an "emotional problem" label is that they get the wrong type of treatment from the mental health professional who is not conversant with alcoholism. In a related example, Davis observes that while whites are as likely as blacks to be alcoholics, the normalization of alcoholism among black subcultures leads to less labeling and therefore the failure to link many black compulsive drinkers to the health-care system. The result is that "the higher proportion of Blacks who die from their alcohol abuse is an outcome of the absence of official labeling and lack of corrective action that may follow such labeling."[13] One could argue with Davis' assertion in that even if blacks and whites received the same frequency of labeling, the rate of black deaths from alcohol abuse would continue to be higher than whites due to the variation in quality of medical care received. One should not, however, dismiss Davis' position that proper labeling can lead to corrective treatment.

In our view, labels as symbols of deviant states and conditions should be demystified. They serve variously as diagnoses, as eligibility requirements for services, as convenient categories for insurance payments, and as a means for banishing people to institutions. The human service professional should face squarely the problems inherent in labeling others and not assume automatically that benefits will accrue from labeling activity.

Generally, there are four assumptions under which human service professionals operate when they label others:

1. Labeling, like diagnosis, is viewed as illuminating and defining a problematic condition presented by the client that provides an identity to a state that exists independently of the label. In other words, the condition being labeled is objectively given.
2. The label itself has no effect on the condition or the individual who is labeled. It is a professional's definition of a state that subsequently will lead to a specific course or sequence of treatment. Furthermore, the label in most contexts is intended to be temporary.
3. The professional who ascribes the label need have little concern for the layman's interpretations, community stigmatizing, or other reactions external to the labeling/treatment situation. Events and factors in these locales are secondary and uncontrollable; persons who respond negatively to clients' labels are ignorant and, therefore, can be ignored. The integrity of a professional's labeling is not to be vitiated or influenced by public stereotypes.

4. Following labeling and corrective treatment, relabeling will occur. The treatment, when left entirely in the hands of the professional, joined with the complete cooperation of the client will eventually produce cure or remediation. Following this, the exdeviant is to become a former mental patient, educated retardate, adjusted exfelon, or recovered alcoholic—a person who can assume a proper role in the community.

As we have seen in Chapters 4 and 5, none of these assumptions are valid. The bestowing of labels is based on subjective criteria, and there is no necessary connection between the label and the treatment. Furthermore, as Richard Stuart has pointed out, "Once a negative label has been applied, there is a clear and present danger that the person so identified will be the victim of additional negative inference solely on the basis of his having been designated as a deviant, without reference either to the behavior that culminated in his having been labeled or to any subsequent actions on his part."[14] There is a tendency for individuals so labeled to organize their lives around the consequences of the stigma they experience from both external and internal sources. Stigma tends to be a continuing process and even if relabeling were to occur, the public does not accept the returning exdeviant as "normal." Phrases such as once a junkie, always a junkie, and once an alcoholic, always an alcoholic are indicators of the pervasiveness of stereotypes and lack of acceptance of the reformed deviant by the public.

In a very thorough review of the literature on public attitudes toward mental illness, Judith Rabkin concludes with the statement:

> The public was less quick than mental health professionals to label odd or deviant behavior as mental illness, but once the label was assigned, either by the community or by professionals, the response was characteristically negative and rejecting. It was widely felt that the mentally ill were rather hopelessly troubled people who probably could not be rescued but who were not terribly worthwhile to begin with. The label of mental illness usually led to irreversibly diminished standing in the eyes of the community, a circumstance that, of course, exacerbated whatever problems of adjustment were initially present.[15]

The assumption that labeling leads to corrective treatment has been widely criticized in both the sociological and psychological literature. For our purposes we have subsumed these criticisms under a separate topic that is termed "label bias."

DISPENSING LABELS: THE PROBLEM OF LABEL BIAS

The dispensing of labels is intended to be a value-free activity accomplished by neutral professionals. When a physician notes that someone has a venereal disease, such as syphilis, he or she has firm knowledge that it is a chronic, infectious disease caused by a spirochete, that there exists an established and agreed upon means of detection, and the disease has a known course of progression if not treated. All of this will be true whether the person the sample has been drawn from lives in a condominium in Fort Lauderdale or a hut in the slums outside Buenos Aires. The total knowledge concerning the origin, nature, course, complications, and treatment of the disease is termed "syphilology."[16] The physician's attitudes about persons who contract syphilis do not enter into his or her judgement about its presence in a particular patient. Should the physician refuse to treat the patient or abuse the individual during treatment, then we can assume that subjective value judgements have been introduced. When this happens, it is not the science of medicine that is at fault but the perspectives and behavior of the physician.

The validity of classifications, categories, and labels dispensed by human service professionals are far more tenuous. Opportunities for interpretation are greater because such professionals are not diagnosing physiological conditions utilizing standard chemical or physical tests but are instead investigating social behaviors. These investigations are apt to be subjective because they are based upon personal observations by human service professionals, or reports received by them, which have few standardized referents. Where standardized formulas exist, as in IQ testing, other factors may intervene that have not been accounted for such as ethnicity and language differences. The state of the art of accurate label dispensing by human service professionals is simply not very good. When a label dispenser is developing a diagnosis, it is presumed that his or her inferences are based upon available evidence that may consist of observations of behavior, interviews in which relevant questions are posed, and psychological tests. Additional factors such as reports, impressions and feelings of others may influence diagnosis, but these should not override inferences built upon information gained through observations, interviews, and tests. Label bias is when the labeler is influenced by irrelevant factors into providing a false diagnosis.

M. K. Temerlin conducted an experiment that exemplifies the potential for label bias. He had ninety-five clinical psychologists, psychiatrists, and graduate students in clinical psychology listen to a tape-recorded interview of an actor who was portraying a mentally healthy man. Prior to listening to the interview half of the subjects were told that a prestigious person in their field had said that the man was psychotic. The control group was not offered this interpretation. While none of the control subjects thought the man was psychotic, 60 percent of the psychiatrists, 28 percent of the clinical psychologists, and 11 percent of the graduate students in the experimental groups diagnosed the man as psychotic. Therefore, one finding of this study was that the suggestion of psychosis by a prestigious individual can increase the likelihood of that diagnosis occurring.[17]

Implications of this study for those human service professionals who function in the mental health sector are particularly disquieting since the field is stratified in a way that locates psychiatrists as "prestigious" persons. While psychologists in general hold no special allegiance to psychiatrists, the same cannot be said of social workers who function in these settings. For a variety of reasons, which will not be dealt with here, it is apparent that social workers, unlike psychologists, are very likely to be subject to label bias when it is a psychiatrist who has previously labeled a client. Furthermore, it can reasonably be anticipated that the Diagnostic and Statistical Manual-III will be increasingly utilized in mental hospitals and community mental health agencies throughout the United States, and many of these settings employ social workers. Since this diagnostic classification scheme was developed by psychiatrists, it is fairly evident that they will be called upon to interpret it relative to specific case diagnoses, thereby increasing the probability of label bias by social workers.

The quality of available stereotypes is another factor that can negatively influence correct labeling by the human service professional. In part, one explanation for the professionals' reliance on these stereotypical judgements has to do with the nature of the domain within which they function. They are involved in intervention and management of the social and psychological dimensions of interpersonal relations. Since this arena does not have health and disease as its central focus but behavior that is to be judged, human service professionals are left to their own devices and subjective interpretations in detecting malfunctioning. Frequently, the theories professionals utilize to fill the vacuum and support their labeling designations are so weak that they resemble ideologies.

One characteristic of an ideology is that it is not vulnerable to challenge or to being disproven. For example, one investigator, Charles S. Suchar, conducted a study that examined a cycle of labeling in a state-run mental health clinic for emotionally disturbed children. The case files of seventeen children, aged six to twelve, were examined. The children were variously labeled schizophrenic, psychotic, or as having character disorders. Suchar discovered that interviews were accomplished with only the parents being present (not the children) and that in all cases the problem was identified as rising from early parent–child relationships. The parents were labeled co-patients, and the state of their mental health was questioned by the therapists. The more the parents were considered to be disturbed, the more the child was assumed to be disturbed. In this way the entire process became cyclical. The child's reported deviant behavior resulted in a label for the child and the labeling of the parents as co-deviants, which led to increased expectations of deviance in the child. The process was set into motion when the parents entered the clinic and reported the child to be a problem. This resulted in an almost automatic labeling of both child and parents. As a result of the professionals' preconceived notions about the cause of mental illness in children, they labeled the parents as deviant for contributing to the child's illness. Then, the professionals sought evidence to support this conjecture. Furthermore, they revised expectations of the child's behavior based on the parent's label.[18]

The problem of erroneous judgements by professionals would

be considerably less serious if they were usually revised when new information became available. In Stanley L. Witkin's review of research on this issue, he found that there was a particular problem of "perseverence" in maintaining initial judgements by human service professionals and that these judgements are usually bound to a theory of behavior.[19]

Witkin reports a study involving thirty-two social workers who viewed the same videotaped interview of a person labeled as shopper or patient. The social workers, following the observation, completed an evaluation questionnaire on the person seen. Among the items presented was a question concerning the most appropriate referral service for this individual, which included choices of mental health, vocational, and general community services.

> Results indicated that when the person was labeled as a patient, social workers were more likely to refer him to a mental health service than when he was labeled as a shopper. However, when asked to assess the impact of various factors on their judgement, workers rated their knowledge of the person as a shopper or patient as having very little influence on their referral choice and significantly less influence than the person's gestures and mannerisms. . . . [20]

In other words, professionals tend to fail to recognize the possibility of label bias in their own diagnoses and justify themselves by reference to insights about persons that may not be valid. Witkin observes that the practitioner, "unaware of this cognitive blind spot . . . may overlook less obvious data predictive of a client's behavior in favor of less useful information consistent with his or her causal theory."[21]

Ethnocentrism, the belief in the superiority of one's own ethnic group, is another factor that may contribute to label bias. This is particularly problematic in the United States due to the heterogeneity of the population being labeled and the homogeneity of the labelers. Minority group members, particularly minorities of color, tend to be disproportionately represented in categories of deviance. Blacks appear to be particularly vulnerable to receiving the harshest or most severe type of labels. J. Zubin and B. Spring reviewed a number of studies that indicate that blacks from all socioeconomic levels emerge from the diagnostic process appearing more disturbed and pathological than whites who exhibit the same behavior.[22] Once they seek or are referred to mental health facilities blacks are apt to be hospitalized for longer periods of time. Furthermore, blacks are evaluated as being more severely disturbed with a poorer prognosis than white patients.

Kent S. Miller reviewed numerous studies in an effort to account for sharply divergent outcomes in incompetency proceedings. Probate courts, in these proceedings, determine if an individual is competent or incompetent following an assessment of his or her mental state. If the individual is found to be incompetent, he or she is committed to a mental hospital. Miller found that personal characteristics rather than behavior, including violence, are predictive of outcomes in incompetency proceedings. Being an unemployed black is very strongly related to a determination of incompetency; males escape incompetency findings twice as often as females, and single or widowed black females fare the worst. Miller's view is that social power is related to the outcome of incompetency proceedings and those with less of it, that is black, elderly, females, are likely to be declared incompetent.[23]

It can be argued that blacks, for a number of reasons, do not avail themselves of psychiatric assistance on as widespread a basis or as often as whites do. Therefore, when they do receive such help their conditions are likely to have deteriorated. More severe labeling and longer hospital stays are the results. However, other investigators have found that the pattern of severe labeling and out-of-home placement exists across human service systems. Sandra M. Stehno, through an analysis of official data and national surveys explored the higher rates of severe labeling and consequent placement of minority children in the child welfare, juvenile court, and mental health systems. She found that while black children were about 15 percent of the total population of youth under age eighteen, they were about 30 percent of those in foster homes and residential group care, and 28.5 percent of those in correctional facilities, and, "of the youths admitted to state and county mental hospitals and inpatient psychiatric units of general hospitals, 27.5 percent were non-white."[24]

Label bias appears to affect minority group members more severely and is one factor that leads to a higher level of placement than is found for whites across human service systems. In regard to the mental health system, Madison Foster and Louis A. Ferman observe that one cause may be that, "The salient anomaly in the field of mental health is that much of the population being served, notably in public institutions, is composed of minority group members while the service providers are non-minority group members." This situation is "further compounded by the general underutilization of the available mental health services by most minority communities." The authors go on to report that while between 17 to 20 percent of the total population is minority (blacks, Hispanics, Asian Americans, and Native Americans) only 8 percent of the American Psychiatric Association membership is. Minority membership in the professional social workers' organization is a bit better than that for psychiatrists, notably 11.4 percent, while the professional psychologists' organization does far worse with a minority membership of only 2.1 percent.[25]

The processes that ensue within the contexts of white professionals labeling blacks are exceedingly difficult to determine. How much of the disproportionate results are due to bias as opposed to the effects of harsh environments is unknown. In a discussion of the literature on this issue, Judith G. Rabkin and Elmer L. Struening observe that "it is generally acknowledged that psychiatric disorders are not distributed randomly throughout the population but tend to be concentrated within definable subgroups" and that "those occupying lower status positions have markedly higher rates of psychiatric disorder."[26] However, as the labeling theorists have argued, it is not the presence of an individual's disorder that leads to labeling and hospitalization but what people make of it that seems to be the crucial factor.

William A. Rushing and Jack Esco present a "status resource hypothesis" to account for the disproportionate number of powerless persons who are to be found in mental hospitals. The hypothesis states that individuals with more resources are better able to control their fates and hence to resist legal coercion that would lead to placement or hospitalization. That is, individuals with higher socioeconomic status have greater resources to attain and maintain desired social status.[27] Rushing and Esco's study suggests that deviance such as mental disorders and social characteristics interact to yield more severe labels, higher rates of placement and longer stays in institutions for minority group members and others with few status resources.

OVERPREDICTING DEVIANCE

Perhaps the single most important problem created by the labelers is that of mislabeling. One type of mislabeling is when ordinary human errors occur, symptoms are confused, or inadequate testing has been performed. Such eventualities can be expected in any technical work. An even more problematic form of mislabeling is due to overprediction since labelers are prone to err on the side of finding deviance rather than not "catching" it. What we have then are "innocent" persons who are designated as deviant without these persons having any way to prove their innocence.

This tendency or proneness to overprediction is a consequence of human service professionals' use of a "medical model" to diagnose the presence or absence of deviant conditions and states. If one examines the procedures that psychiatrists use, one will find that a frequent error in psychiatric diagnosis is overprediction of deviance, that is, a bias toward false positives. A false positive occurs when someone is assumed to have a disease, and it turns out later that the person does not. False positives occur frequently in the practice of medicine, since physicians attempt to discover if certain symptoms are being caused by underlying pathological processes. Subjecting patients to medical tests may cause them inconvenience and are likely to be expensive but rarely do they cause actual harm. In psychiatry, however, a bias toward false positives results in people being labeled mentally ill when they are normal.

In an article dealing with reliability in the prediction of suicide, Richard D. Kaplan and others examined the behavior of clinicians who examine and assess potentially suicidal patients. The authors point out that, "because a false negative assessment [mistaking a suicidal person for a nonsuicidal person] of suicide risk has fatal consequences, psychiatrists are more comfortable with false positive than false negative diagnoses. Medical tradition in general tends to accept false positive diagnosis when the treatment is perceived as relatively benign and the danger of untreated illness is great."[28] Of course, the decision that a person is suicidal may lead to involuntary hospitalization that is accomplished by a relatively low standard of proof, such as the therapist's suspicions that the person is suicidal.[29]

An interesting feature of predicting deviance in a manner that leads to an overabundance of false positives is that the more one overpredicts the more likely one is to come up with true positives. That is, if we were to study 100 children and predict that they would all become delinquent, we would then have correctly predicted the seven or eight who actually do. Our errors would be the ninety-two or ninety-three children who do not become delinquent. However, people who engage in labeling professionally tend to discount their false positive predictions, primarily because they fail to see their efforts as being harmful.

A bias towards false positives among professionals may affect minorities, women, and the elderly disproportionately, since they tend to have less influence in the labeling process throughout all the service systems than others. Ethnocentrism coupled with a bias towards false positives by professionals creates a situation of double jeopardy for blacks and other powerless persons. Their differences are more likely to be construed as manifestations of abnormality rather than eccentricity; just to be on the safe side, such persons are labeled mentally ill.

These practices, while perhaps being most glaring in regard to the labeling of minorities, are extended to other populations that vary from an idealized norm of middle class America. For example, William Rushing examined the records of first-time admissions of three state psychiatric hospitals over a ten year period. He categorized and classified each individual in one of three marital categories, married, disrupted-estranged, and single. The findings of the research indicated that "the involuntary/voluntary [commitment] ratio increases as socioeconomic status decreases." That is, poor people are more likely to be involuntarily committed. A similar pattern was found to be the case for marital status in that the order of the involuntary/voluntary ratios moved from single, disrupted-estranged, and married. Rushing concludes his study with the observation that social and economic resources and degree of community integration are significant contingencies in the tendency to hospitalize people involuntarily.[30]

A somewhat similar type of false positive determination was found by Mercer to affect Mexican–American school children in the city of Riverside, California. As a consequence of administering a single intelligence test to all children in the public schools, Mexican–American pupils were labeled retarded in numbers disproportionate to their percentage in the total population. Mexican–American children, who made up 9.5 percent of the school population constituted almost a third of all pupils labeled retarded. White pupils who made up 82 percent of the school population contributed only 54 percent of the retardates. One of Mercer's findings is particularly consistent with the overprediction feature of the medical model, that is, a single symptom is sufficient to designate suspected abnormality. She found that Mexican–Americans holding the status of mental retardate are less deviant than "Anglos" holding that status. In other words, Mexican–American children labeled as retarded have higher IQ test scores and fewer physical disabilities than Anglos similarly labeled. Furthermore, situational retardation is more common among Mexican–American children, that is, it is not a comprehensive status but one that appears mainly in the public schools.[31]

Other critics of the way in which professionals label point out that children are particularly vulnerable to being caught up in the overprediction problem.* In part, this is because the arena for detecting deviation in children is the public school which, in attending to its goals, frequently emphasizes control as a means. Since schools are engaged in the congregate management of only partially socialized human beings, sorting of pupils into categories is a standard means of locating and handling deviations. Indeed, the successes achieved in utilizing schools as the locale for testing children for difficulties in hearing and vision has been notable. Similar efforts to detect hyperkinetic children have led to overidentification since this label is a convenient one and enlists the aid of physicians and parents in controlling children in the

---

*See, for example. Peter Schrag and Diane Divoky, *The Myth of the Hyperactive Child* (New York: Pantheon Books, Inc., 1975); Peter Conrad and Joseph Schneider, *Deviance and Medicalization* (St. Louis, Missouri: The C. V. Mosby Company, 1980).

schools. One expert in the area stresses that greater caution should be exercised:

> In fact, a current fad in some quarters attributes all school behavior problems to "minimal brain dysfunction", "neurological handicap", "hyper-activity", "hyperkinetic syndrome", or whatever other diagnostic label is used to describe the handicap.... The prevalence rate of four percent can often help decide doubtful situations. For example, if a school already has 15 percent of its students diagnosed and/or medicated, the probability that another child should be so diagnosed plummets to near zero. The pool of undiagnosed hyperkinetics in that school should be exhausted already.... Although teachers are usually the best source of objective observations about a child's behavior and performance, some judgement must be exercised in accepting those observations. Sometimes it seems that the advisability of diagnosing [and medicating] a given child varies inversely with his teacher's enthusiasm for it. The teacher who is unwilling to admit the child is abnormal, only reluctantly asks for help, and may even be prejudiced against medication is likely describing a hyperkinetic child even when trying to hide the fact. By contrast, the teacher who can cite a half-dozen children in his randomly grouped class to illustrate the benefits of medication and is convinced that he has found another hyperkinetic child should arouse some skepticism about the label he is trying to paste on the child.[32]

Human service professionals appear to invoke personal judgements of what is normative when they apply labels to people. Such personal judgements often reflect the professional's own background and outlook on life as well as the theory of human behavior he or she prefers. Factors such as social class, ethnicity, and gender, which should be irrelevant, may then be brought into play in influencing the labeling designation. The use of various tests and classification schemes by professionals may serve to reduce the introduction of irrelevant criteria in labeling situations, but many of these devices are composed by persons who share ethnocentric biases or are based on norms that exclude an appreciation of cultural differences. One psychiatrist, James Robitscher, indicates that intelligence testing has been widely criticized for cultural bias, for causing premature closure, and for not testing intelligence but instead measuring the ability to take a particular kind of examination.[33]

It should be evident that the problems of label bias and over-prediction are largely systemic and represent key problems in the social reaction to human deviations. Yet, like most human problems, these too are interactional, and there are some steps that individual practitioners can take to counteract them. Clearly, it is desirable for the human service professional to avoid or reduce the effects of their own distortions, label bias, and overprediction. Witkin proposes five steps that could help accomplish this:

1. Increased awareness of the nature of biases may lessen the professional's susceptibility to them.
2. By developing greater empathy, the professional is able to view the world from the client's perspective. "A simple but effective method of reducing actor–observer differences would be for practitioners to assume the client's role periodically."
3. A knowledge of statistical concepts such as sampling and probability would be helpful to the professional. For example, "an extreme performance [by a child] on a particular day is probably not an accurate predictor of the next day's performance."
4. "The utilization of multiple sources of data for evaluating the functioning of clients. Such sources include different observers, different settings, and different areas of performance."
5. The professional should seek to collect data or make observations "in other areas of the client's life not specifically targeted for intervention" that could be useful in determining assets and strengths.[34]

All of these are useful suggestions for guiding the work of human service professionals and reducing distortions that have their sources in the professional and personal perspectives of the practitioner. However, another source of difficulty, which has been alluded to earlier in this book, is the interaction of professionals and the human service organizations in which they work.

ORGANIZATIONAL PROCESSING OF DEVIANTS

Typically, when one thinks of organizations within the context of the study of deviance such institutions as prisons and mental hospitals come to mind. However, organizations are far more pervasive in all our lives. It has been noted that

> One of the hallmarks of the modern society has been the vast proliferation of formal organizations explicitly designed to process and change people. This trend reflects, on the one hand, the shift of socialization and social control functions from primary groups such as the family to the state; on the other hand, it reflects the development of complex people-processing and people-changing techniques that can no longer be implemented in small social units.
>
> Inevitably, every person conducts transactions, voluntarily or involuntarily, with a whole range of organizations whose explicit purpose is to shape, change, and control his behavior as well as confirm or redefine his social and personal status.[35]

Organizations that we all come into contact with and that seek to change us in some manner include the public schools, hospitals, and churches.

Then what is the connection between organizations and deviance? For one thing, as has been noted by Edwin M. Schur, "organizations produce deviants."[36] As has been stated earlier, labels only become official statuses through the activities and processes of human service organizations. The dispensing of labels is, in a sense, both an activity engaged in by and a product of an organization. Mental hospitals take in disturbing persons and discharge the disturbed— persons labeled as having had some form of mental disorder. Juvenile courts receive misbehaving children and transform them into adjudicated delinquents. Some human service organizations can be perceived as deviance manufacturing concerns, taking in formless and undifferentiated material and putting out defined and recognizable (but deviant) products. Others seek to produce a more normal product, such as graduates of technical or vocational schools. Still other organizations, such as public schools, do both.

In this section I intend to examine (a) the requirement for many human service organizations to utilize professionals to validate their activities, (b) the routinization of labeling within these organizations, and (c) how organizational imperatives influence labeling.

The mental hospital and the reformatory are human service organizations, as are the public school, community mental health center, and the residential facility or group home for retarded adults. One distinction between the prison, the juvenile training school, and other human service organizations is the sanctioned use of coercive-repressive measures to promote conformity and change in the deviant–client. Labeling theorists and others have seized upon the manner in which deviants are handled in these settings, depicting such organizations as uniformly oppressive. While these analyses have contributed to an understanding of the institution as punitive, in the popular mind this type of organization remains an exception. If institutions are "bad" then community-based agencies and services must therefore be "good." However, in reality, there are certain similarities between coercive-repressive organizations and those that attempt to meet their goals through normative means. Schools can be enlightened learning environments with highly positive relations between pupils and teachers or disciplinary institutions in which pupils are under constant surveillance and threatened with physical punishment for any infraction. Both the normative organization and the coercive-repressive one receive, screen, define, and manage deviants.

There are also differences between these two types of organizations. Far less attention has been given to an examination of those organizations utilizing a normative compliance base where coercion is replaced by efforts at persuasive communication. The family service agency, community mental health center, physical rehabilitation workshop, and other organizations offering voluntary counseling services can be classified as normative organizations that rely upon the cooperation of their clients. One distinction between the coercive-repressive and normative organization is the variation in standardization between the two. Standardization, in this context, refers to how clients are processed and the rigidity or flexibility of the treatment sequence. The degree of standardization is related to a conception the organization has of its clients, particularly its view of the clients' cooperativeness, and a more general picture of human behavior and its complexities. Normative organizations tend toward less standardization than coercive-repressive ones, emphasize uniqueness of clients rather than similarities, and see them as being generally malleable.[37]

What is the contribution of the normative human service organization to the creation of deviant identities through labeling? For

one thing, it is those characteristics identified above that lead
normative organizations increasingly to rely upon professionals to
carry forward their technologies in attempting to meet their goals.
Where coercion has given way to persuasion as a predominant
means for achieving control over clients, specialists in persuasive
communication tend to assume both core and elite positions in
these organizations. The key theme of this communication is to
have the client believe that it is in his or her best interests to
cooperate as fully as possible. In this way suggestions may carry
the force of demands with far less effort being expended and little
resentment being produced.

In rationalizing their ascendant roles in normative organizations,
these specialists stress the complexity of human behavior and the
associated difficulties involved in mounting strategies directed at
changing it. The more complex the task, it is argued, the more
specialized skills and training are needed. In defining clients as
being seriously ill, difficult, and profoundly disturbed, justification for professional expertise is achieved. Just as elite medical
centers announce that within their operating rooms more open
heart surgery is performed than appendectomies, there are advan-
tages to human service organizations' claims that their clients are
not average cases but severely involved ones. Organizations' names
are changed to keep pace with the new images desired. In this way
the orphan asylum becomes the residential treatment center and
the institution for the insane becomes the neuropsychiatric institute.
One consequence, therefore, of professionalizing human service
organizations is the tendency toward more severe labeling.

In addition, in the absence of concrete evidence of organizational accomplishments, the presence of professionals can be pointed
to as an approximate validation of program achievements. For
example, the residential home for children with a full comple-
ment of professional staff and a consulting psychiatrist can claim a
level of psychological expertise that similar organizations without
these specialists cannot. One artifact in asserting the availability
and utilization of psychological expertise is that it must be played
against very complex problems in human behavior. Such expertise has no particular relevance for normals, at least in the eyes of
the public. Lastly, it is the professionals who are seen as possessing

the technical skills and knowledge required for diagnosis and accurate labeling of complicated human frailty.

In these ways, justification builds on rationalization. For example, in the children's services field one hears the refrain, the kids sent to us are getting worse, meaning each year the cases are more involved and disorganized or the children are acting out more radically. This sets the stage for requests by these agencies for additional professional staff and involves them in developing more elaborate treatment procedures and even more intricate screening. As this process unfolds, the incidence of severe labeling becomes even more pronounced.

What leads human service professionals, who in their various codes of ethics espouse a primary commitment to clients, to contribute to the perpetuation of deviance and to help persons embark on deviant careers? Does the professional truly believe that labeling someone a "character disorder" or a "paranoid schizophrenic" will, as events unfold, really help that person? That is, even in those cases where labeling cannot lead to corrective treatment, professionals will continue to label. The question is why?

Hasenfeld, in discussing the sources of professional power offers two reasons. One reflects a type of contract that exists between the state and professionals that is rarely discussed but is well understood by both parties. Professionals, as a group, are given exclusive rights by the state, through certification and licensing, to work with various populations so long as they control deviants and maintain dominant values. So while labeling may not lead to a person receiving help, it can contribute to his or her eventual control.[38] Second, professional authority is not precisely the same as administrative or bureaucratic authority. Professionals are prone to point out that administrative authority interferes with the performance of their work. As Hasenfeld observes, human service professionals "are subject to greater organizational evaluation and administrative authority and have less control over the content and conditions of their work" than do lawyers and doctors.[39] Therefore, their freedom to exercise choice in the decision to label or not label is limited.

Would professionals then, if left to their own devices, engage in less labeling? It is doubtful that this would happen since labeling is both an organizational and a professional activity. Hasenfeld, in commenting on the potential conflict between professional autonomy and bureaucratic authority notes: "However, such a conflict may be more imaginary than real if it is recognized that both bureaucratization and professionalism are alternate mechanisms of control. Through bureaucratization, the organization relies on task specification, routinization, and formalization of procedures to set limits on staff performance. Through professionalism, the organization relies on internalized professional standards and norms to set such limits."[40]

In fact, professionals not only perform tasks that the organization seeks to have accomplished, they mold the organization to their own particular perspectives. In seeking to infuse the organization with their perspectives, and achieve dominance by doing so, professionals attempt to exact a moderate degree of bureaucratization. Freidson states the case very well in observing that "As a special kind of occupation, professionals have attempted to solve the problems of persuasion by obtaining institutional powers and prerogatives which at the very least set limits on the freedom of their prospective clients, and which on occasion even coerce their clients into compliance. The expertise of the professional is institutionalized into something similar to bureaucratic office."[41]

Located within the "intake" or diagnostic units of many human service organizations are some of the more confounding features of the conjoining of professional expertise and bureaucratic organization. In place of a needed triage system useful for differentiating among cases requiring varying degrees of attention and care, we find a routinization of labeling and treatment procedures based on factors irrelevant to client needs. Inflexible rules are established that are based on principles derived from theories of personality or that serve to promote exemplary professional performance. The rules, when strictly observed, serve to deny the individuality of the client and promote bureaucratic handling. Suchar's findings, for example, reported earlier in this chapter, revealed that parents who brought their children to a clinic for treatment were labeled along with their children. This is not an unusual occurrence. Many child guidance clinics and family service agencies require that parents be seen in therapy although the parents' intention is to have only the child treated. The parents, believing that they are helping their child by agreeing to participate, become clients of the agency. This rule most likely emerges out of the belief of professionals that parents somehow not only contribute to the problems experienced by children, but they arrange for their child to behave in deviant ways. The rule is implemented even in the face of evidence to the contrary, such as the discovery that the child's problems are caused by interactions with peers or unusual school pressures.

Another rule, one found in many voluntary agencies, is that clients are expected to wait their turn for service. The agency, in this example, establishes a waiting list thereby emphasizing a concept of fairness rather than professional judgement about the severity of different clients' problems. One rationale offered for this type of procedure is that only well-motivated clients are willing to wait for service while others less motivated will drop out of the waiting list. Placing an emphasis upon motivation rather than the severity of the problem reflects the agency's interest in exemplary professional practice rather than serving those most in need.

Earlier in this chapter we discussed one outcome of the education of human service professionals—the production of false positive labeling. One source of this type of error is the use of a medical model in approaching problems of deviance. The rule that is used when uncertainty arises is to continue to suspect illness or deviance even when the bulk of the evidence points in another direction. The tendency toward false positive labeling is a bias of human service professionals that is congruent with certain imperatives facing the organization in which they are employed. Of primary importance is the need of organizational elites to avoid external criticism of themselves and of their organization. In the case of courts and mental hospitals, the tendency toward false positives will lead to an overidentification of the presence of mental illness and the underidentification of recovered patients. David Mechanic[42] and Thomas J. Scheff,[43] in separate works, have concluded that psychiatrists who screen incoming mental patients often operate with a presumption of mental illness. Scheff goes on to note that "The policy of presuming illness is probably both cause and effect of, political pressure on the court from the community. The judge, an elected official, runs the risk of being more heavily penalized for erroneously releasing than for erroneously retaining patients. Since the judge personally appoints the panel of psychiatrists to serve as examiners, he can easily transmit the community pressure to them, by failing to reappoint a psychiatrist whose examinations were inconveniently thorough."

A study that has received an extraordinary amount of attention by social scientists and criticism by psychiatrists was performed by D. L. Rosenham. He had eight normal people attempt to gain admission to twelve public and private mental hospitals throughout the United States. Among the group of pseudopatients were the author, and three other psychologists, a pediatrician, a psychiatrist, a painter, and a housewife. Upon appearing at the hospital, each pseudopatient feigned the single symptom that he or she was hearing voices. Following this, each pseudopatient cooperated with hospital personnel, offered their true case histories when asked, and following admission "behaved on the ward as he (or she) 'normally' behaved." Of the twelve diagnoses provided at the different hospitals, eleven were schizophrenic and one was manic-depressive psychosis. "Length of hospitalization ranged from 7 to 52 days, with an average of 19 days." While the outcome of this study exemplifies the inclination among psychiatrists to make false positive predictions, thereby overpredicting mental illness, the author cites the mental hospital environment as conducive to diagnostic error and, subsequently, promoting the failure to perceive pseudopatients acting normally as normal.[44]

Additional aspects of Rosenham's data indicate the following:

The pseudopatients received more than 2,100 pills.

In all cases, the diagnosis at discharge was schizophrenia in remission.

Other patients voiced suspicions that the pseudopatients were actually pseudopatients, either journalists or professors.[45]

The various findings presented in this study suggest that the designation of labels by psychiatrists in mental hospitals is routinized, with the shaping of systematic machinery for moving patients from one stage to the next.[46] In order to accomplish this type of routinization, organizational operatives must stereotype the individuals to be moved along. A single characteristic shared by all pseudopatients in the Rosenham study was that of reported hallucinations. Since this symptom may indicate the presence of schizophrenia and since that illness accounts for the largest number of persons admitted to mental hospitals in the United States, then it is assumed that these patients must have that condition. We have no way of truly knowing if this type of reductionism actually occurred during the Rosenham study, but the persistence of a high error rate in overpredicting schizophrenia, was also found by Taylor and Abrams[47] and discussed by Robitscher: "The national range of incidence of schizophrenia in patients admitted to mental hospitals is 24 percent but a research study that applied rigorous criteria that included formal thought disorder, emotional blunting, hallucinations or delusions . . . found only a 6 percent rate. The authors of the study say that there was a fivefold overdiagnosis of schizophrenia in the hospitals and clinics where the research was conducted.[48]

In the studies cited above it is difficult to detect how much of the label bias realized can be attributed to routinization, stereotyping, or the effect of organizational imperatives. As Rosenham notes "it is clearly more dangerous to misdiagnose illness than health. Better to err on the side of caution, to suspect illness even among the healthy."[49] Such patterns can be attributed to the humane concern of psychiatrists for their patients or alternately, be conceived of as hospital employees trying to protect themselves and their organizations.

In his classic article on goal displacement by agencies established to serve the blind, Scott attributes label bias directly to organizational imperatives. Such agencies seek young, intelligent, blind persons who can be educated and employed and tend to hold on to them, "sequestre" them and correspondingly neglect older blind persons. Scott notes that the proliferation of services for a limited segment of the blind population is due to numerous and complex reasons but concludes "the programs and services for the blind are often more responsive to the organizational needs of agencies through which services are offered, then they are to the needs of blind persons."[50] Presumably, in Scott's example, the organization is acting in a rational manner, that in selecting the capable blind for service the bias eventuates in exactly what was intended, exemplary organizational performance. However, a large majority of the blind in the United States do not fit the characteristics these organizations seek and are therefore unserved or underserved.

As we have seen, the labeling of clients by human service organizations tends to serve a multiplicity of purposes and is further influenced by the belief systems of professionals. As human service organizations professionalize, they tend to become infused with the perspectives and aspirations of professionals which, in turn, may determine the rate of deviance production. In Mercer's California study, for example, the professionalized public schools, which utilized diagnosticians and other specialists, produced a high rate of mentally retarded pupils especially among the Mexican–American population. The Catholic parochial schools in the same city produced an extremely low rate of mentally retarded pupils. The Catholic parochial schools, unlike the public schools, had no special classes for the mentally retarded and no achievement or ability testing program. Out of 2,800 children attending these schools, two were identified as retarded and both had observable physical anomalies.[51]

It can be argued that parochial schools, not having facilities and programs to educate the retarded, detect such cases and refuse to admit them or refer them on to the public schools. But this seems not to be the case. When tested, twenty-seven parochial school pupils (1.1% of population) had an IQ test score of seventy-nine or below and would have been eligible for the status of mental retardate had they attended public schools. In the parochial schools they were normal students although teachers perceived them as children with academic problems.[52]

Similarly, whether or not a child is designated "learning disabled" is highly dependent on the perspectives of the school in which the pupil is enrolled. The diagnosis of learning disability is arrived at by exclusion and discrepancy rather than the presence of symptoms.

"Learning disability is generally diagnosed by the exclusion of negative neurological, social, and psychoemotional etiology and by a significant discrepancy between levels of intellectual as compared with academic achievement." While the type of balancing act required of the diagnostician by these criteria is accomplishable, it is the school system that introduces the pertinent standard. Rachel Gittelman terms this "the elusive expectation factor" wherein a school system that considers a two-year deficit in reading or mathematics as acceptable is not going to find as many learning disabled children as one that insists upon parity with a national average.[53]

The various research findings noted above indicate high error rates in labeling persons as deviant and the corruption of the labeling process through narrow professional perspectives and the instrusion of organizational imperatives. Just the same, it should be recognized that the delivery of services to those in need, deviant or otherwise, is preceded by some form of labeling, be it diagnosis, assessment, or the determination of eligibility. That is how services are organized in the United States. Even stereotypes are useful to the extent that the level of practice in the human service organization is not supported by an extensive scientific body of knowledge. Some cautions should be exercised, however, by the responsible professional in order to seek a reduction in the problems inherent in labeling at this time:

1. Recognition and acceptance of the fact that the art of labeling is generally poor.
2. Since inaccuracy in labeling is prevalent, labeled clients should be reassessed periodically to determine if the original label continues to be an appropriate one.
3. Labeled clients, their families, and perhaps their reference groups should not be persuaded or forced to accept the profferred label. Frequently, it is more helpful for other relevant persons to view the client within their own frame of reference and thus make it easier for them to accept him or her.

Systemic oriented remedies to the problems of labeling will be presented in the final chapter.

REFERENCES

1. Bernard A. Thorsell and Lloyd W. Klemke, "The Labeling Process: Reinforcement and Deterrent?" in *Deviant Behavior: Readings in the Sociology of Deviance,* ed. Delos H. Kelly (New York: St. Martin's Press, 1979) pp. 654–55.
2. Arthur Lewis Wood, *Deviant Behavior and Control Strategies* (Lexington, Massachusetts: Lexington Books, D. C. Heath and Company, 1974) p. 3.
3. Morris Janowitz, *The Last Half-Century: Societal Change and Politics in America* (Chicago: The University of Chicago Press, 1978) pp. 28–30.
4. Wood, *Deviant Behavior,* p. 53.
5. Amitai Etzioni, *A Comparative Analysis of Complex Organizations* (New York: The Free Press, 1975) pp. 5–6.
6. Etzioni, *Comparative Analysis,* p. 5.
7. John H. Gagnon and Gerald C. Carison, "Asylums, the Token Economy, and the Metrics of Mental Life," *Behavior Therapy, 7:* 528–34, 1976.
8. Janowitz, *Last Half-Century,* p. 441.
9. Etzioni, *Comparative Analysis,* pp. 5–6.
10. Talcott Parsons, "On the Concept of Influence," *Public Opinion Quarterly, 27* (Spring): 37–52, 1951.
11. Etzioni, *Comparative Analysis,* pp. 10–11.
12. Richard B. Stuart, *Trick or Treatment: How and When Psychotherapy Fails* (Champaign, Ill.: Research Press, 1970).
13. Nanette J. Davis, *Sociological Constructions of Deviance: Perspectives and Issues in the Field* (Dubuque, Iowa: Wm. C. Brown Co., Pub., 1975), pp. 181–182.
14. Stuart, *Trick or Treatment,* p. 104.
15. Judith Rabkin, "Public Attitudes toward Mental Illness: A Review of the Literature," *Schizophrenia Bulletin, 10* (Fall): 28, 1974.
16. William Morris, ed., *The American Heritage Dictionary of the English Language* (Boston: American Heritage Publishing Co., Inc. and Houghton Mifflin Company, 1971).
17. M. K. Temerlin, "Suggestion Effects in Psychiatric Diagnosis," *Journal of Nervous and Mental Disease,* 147: 349–53, 1968.
18. Charles S. Suchar, "The Institutional Reaction to Child Mental Illness: Co-Deviant Labeling," *Journal of Social Issues, 34:* 76–92, 1978.
19. Stanley L. Witkin, "Cognitive Processes in Clinical Practice," *Social Work, 27* (5) (September): 389–95, 1982.
20. Witkin, "Cognitive Processes," 392.
21. Witkin, "Cognitive Processes," 392.
22. J. Zubin and B. Spring, "A New View of Schizophrenia," *Journal of Abnormal Psychology, 88:*2, 1977.
23. Kent S. Miller, *Managing Madness* (New York: The Free Press, 1976) pp. 42–43.
24. Sandra M. Stehno, "Differential Treatment of Minority Children in Service Systems," *Social Work, 27* (1) (January): 39–45, 1982.
25. Madison Foster and Louis A. Ferman, "Minority Populations and Mental

Health Manpower Development: Some Facts of Life" (unpublished paper, University of Michigan, 1979), pp. 2-5.

26. Judith G. Rabkin and Elmer L. Struening, *Ethnicity, Social Class and Mental Illness*, Working Paper Series, Number 17 (New York: Institute on Pluralism and Group Identity, May, 1976) p. 1.

27. William A. Rushing and Jack Esco, "The Status Resource Hypothesis and Length of Hospitalization," in *Deviant Behavior and Social Process* (rev. ed.), ed. William A. Rushing (Chicago: Rand McNally, 1975) pp. 445-55.

28. Richard D. Kaplan and others, "Reliability and Rationality in the Prediction of Suicide," *Hospital and Community Psychiatry, 33* (3) (March): 212-15, 1982.

29. Kaplan, "Reliability and Rationality," p. 215.

30. William A. Rushing, "Individual Resources, Societal Reaction and Hospital Commitment," *The American Journal of Sociology, 77* (Nov.): 511-26, 1971.

31. Jane R. Mercer, Labeling the Mentally Retarded (Berkeley, California: University of California Press, 1973) pp. 98-108.

32. L. Eugene Arnold, "Is This Label Necessary?" *The Journal of School Health, XLIII* (8) (Oct.): 1973 p. 13.

33. Jonas Robitscher, *The Powers of Psychiatry* (Boston, MA: Houghton Mifflin, 1980) p. 216.

34. Witkin, "Cognitive Processes," pp. 393-94.

35. Yeheskel Hasenfeld and Richard A. English, eds., *Human Service Organizations* (Ann Arbor: University of Michigan Press, 1974) p. 1.

36. Edwin M. Schur, *Labeling Deviant Behavior: Its Sociological Implications* (New York: Harper and Row, Publishers, 1971) p. 82.

37. Vinter, "Analysis of Treatment Organizations," in *Human Service Organizations*, eds. Hasenfeld and English, p. 430.

38. Hasenfeld and English, *Human Service Organizations*, p. 162.

39. Hasenfeld and English, *Human Service Organizations*, p. 163.

40. Hasenfeld and English, *Human Service Organizations*, p. 163.

41. Eliot Freidson, "Dominant Professions," in *Human Service Organizations*, eds. Hasenfeld and English, p. 430.

42. David Mechanic, "Some Factors in Identifying and Defining Mental Illness," *Mental Hygiene, 46*:66-74, 1962.

43. Thomas J. Scheff, "The Societal Reaction to Deviance: Ascriptive Elements in the Psychiatric Screening of Mental Patients in a Midwestern State," *Social Problems, II* (4) (Spring): 401-443, 1964.

44. D. L. Rosenhan, "Being Sane in Insane Places," *Science, 179* (January): 250-258, 1973.

45. Rosenhan, "Being Sane in Insane Places," p. 253.

46. Schur, Labeling Deviant Behavior, p. 97.

47. Michael Alan Taylor and Richard Abrams, "The Prevalence of Schizophrenia: A Reassessment Using Modern Diagnostic Criteria," *American Journal of Psychiatry, 135:* 945-48, 1978.

48. Robitscher, *The Powers of Psychiatry.*
49. Rosenhan, "Being Sane in Insane Places," 253.
50. Robert A. Scott, "The Selection of Clients by Social Welfare Agencies: The Case of The Blind," *Social Problems, 14* (Winter): 248–257, 1967.
51. Mercer, Labeling the Mentally Retarded, p. 100.
52. Mercer, Labeling the Mentally Retarded, p. 100.
53. Rachel Gittelman, "Learning Disabilities," *Journal of Child Psychiatry, 19* (4) (Autumn): 547–48, 1980.

Chapter 7

OF MODELS AND REMEDIES

THE LABELING PROFESSIONS

The last few chapters have addressed labeling theory and the implications of that perspective for the responsible human service professional. The various groups that are responsible for identifying, managing, and treating deviants such as psychiatry, psychology, and social work are essentially labeling professions. Professionals in these groups are trained in requisite labeling skills in universities, recognized by state governments through licensing as possessing the expertise to provide these designations, and mandated by human service organizations to perform the tasks involved. All of this is unlikely to change in the near future.

The reader should not conclude from the earlier discussion that the effects of labeling are necessarily always negative. There are occasions when the designation of a label may have positive consequences even when the problem that led to the labeling is not corrected. As a case in point, L. Arnold cites an example of a child newly labeled "hyperkinetic," whereas he had been previously thought of by his teachers and parents as poorly motivated, aggressive, and "just a bad boy." The "hyperkinetic" label was actually an upgrading whereby the child could be seen in a new light. He is now able to be viewed as a frustrated child possessing a handicap that he is endeavoring to overcome. As such, it is easier for people, particularly adults, to be more helpful and less antagonistic and angry with the child. Arnold terms this phenomenon the establishment of a "virtuous circle" wherein people respond to the child with more optimistic expectations, understanding, support, and an increased appreciation for what the child is going through.[1]

The positive outcome identified in this case example is dependent on negative formal and informal labeling preceding the "hyper-

kinetic" label. That is, the new label is only desirable relative to
the negative effects of prior labels. What the "hyperkinetic" label
does in this case is to change the observers' interpretation of the
actor's intent; from wilfull to unwilfull deviance. The individual
is seen as an involuntary actor who has a physiological or neurological problem that has caused the deviant behavior. Such problems fall within the realm of medicine and those professions allied
to it.

THE MEDICAL MODEL

There appear to be two interconnected historical trends that
will continue to influence the roles of the labeling professions.
Both trends are directly related to the changing nature of deviance
definition and control in society. The first is the gradual emergence of a humanitarian trend in the conception and control of
deviance during the twentieth century. In most quarters, deviant
behavior and conditions, such as alcoholism, illegitimacy, and
mental illness, are not thought of as sins, divine retribution, or
possession by evil spirits. An ecclesiastical view of deviance has
been replaced by growing enlightenment regarding deviants and
their behavior. Accompanying this development there has been a
corresponding diminution of retributive perspectives as a response
to deviance. To a considerable extent the public's conviction about
willfulness in deviance is largely reserved for criminal behavior
although the degree of involuntarism in alcoholism and certain
other behaviors is subject to much debate. Coercive control of
many categories of deviant behavior has been replaced by social
control.

The second trend is replacement of the ecclesiastical deviance model with one that views deviance as illness or at least
as a condition of unknown causality that is treatable by medical technology. Conrad and Schneider assess the trend toward
humanitarianism in their analysis of the societal shift in deviance designations that they refer to as "the medicalization of
deviance."[2] They identify five positive effects of "medicalization,"
namely,

1. Medical definitions of deviance "are imbued with the prestige of the medical profession and are considered the 'scientific' and humane way of viewing a problem."
2. "Medicalization allows for the extension of the sick role to those labeled as deviants" thereby removing blame from the individual for his or her behavior.
3. An optimistic view of outcomes is generated since "cure" for most illness is possible; if not immediately then soon since medical "breakthroughs" occur periodically.
4. By placing the problem in the hands of physicians, the prestige of the profession is added to acts of labeling and treatment, thereby validating both.
5. Greater flexibility relative to individual needs of the patient is permissible, as opposed to judicial and legal control, for example, methadone treatment for addicts rather than incarceration. This flexibility also promotes increased efficiency.[3]

In medicalizing deviance, that is, in treating deviance as an illness, an approach to its understanding and remediation is utilized that has been referred to as the "medical model." The meaning of the idea of model, as posed by Wood, is that it is a way of denoting "a configuration of interrelated elements that constitute a systematic way of looking at a process that distinguishes it from alternative configurations."[4]

A model is a conceptual tool useful in examining certain phenomena occurring in the world around us. It should be noted, however, that in practice there are no "pure" models. Medicine is influenced by the market structure in which it is practiced, for example private practice for profit versus socialized medicine. Sociological models are influenced by psychology and vice versa. Both psychologists and sociologists may be influenced by anthropology and economics. On the negative side, as we have seen, biases on the individual level tend to affect label designations by human service professionals. On the organizational level existing models are "modified, distorted, and stretched as efforts are made to mobilize financial and man-power resources and to deal with the daily problems of running ... [an] agency."[5]

The medical model is variously referred to as the "disease" or "treatment" model and is derived from the often successful practice of medicine in the treatment of physical ailments. Actually there are a number of medical models, for example, public health and prevention. In order to keep matters clear, the term medical-illness model will be used in this discussion. There are two key components to the medical-illness model, one having to do with assumptions about the cause of illness; the other having to do with its treatment.

1. *Etiology of illness*
    a. The core is the germ theory of disease. Modern medicine began with the discovery that particular agents, usually microscopic, are the sole cause of certain illnesses.
    b. The doctrine of specific etiology says that a particular disease can be explained by a distinct, well-defined, biochemical or physiological abnormality.
    c. Disease reflects disordered biological mechanisms in the human body that can ultimately be described in terms of chemistry and physics.
    d. The disease theory of sickness maintains that the human experience of being unwell can be explained by a discrete, isolated entity that exists independently of its manifestation in a particular person.[6]

2. *Treatment of the illness*
    a. An effective or ameliorative treatment is known for many types of illnesses, and new discoveries may close the gap even further.
    b. Treatment involves doing something to the person who is afflicted, such as prescribing drugs or undertaking surgery.
    c. The disease condition may get worse, leave permanent damage, or continue for an extended period if the treatment is not administered.
    d. Treatments, even if they do no good, are rarely enduringly harmful to the patient.[7]

There are two other assumptions regarding the medical-illness model that should be explored briefly before we turn to the application of this model to problems of human deviance. One has to do with the confusion between disease and illness that are often thought to be synonomous. A disease is a physiological state of the human organism. Illness, on the other hand, is a social state in which the individual assumes a sick role. The Rosenhan study, discussed earlier, in which confederates feigned mental disorders and were admitted to hospitals and treated as if they were sick, is an example of sick role "playing." Disease was not present.

An inference is made that the disease causes the illness, but in actuality, the two can exist independently. It is possible to have a disease without one assuming a sick role just as it is possible for one to assume a sick role and not have a disease, as in the case of "hysterical" illness. A third possibility exists, that of iatrogenic illness, an illness that is induced in a patient by a physician's words or actions. In other words, there is no necessary connection between illness and disease.

A second assumption underlying the medical-illness model is its implicit definition of normality. Normality is viewed as a residual category, that is, it is noted by the absence of pathological symptoms. The term normal can be used to refer to the absence of disease or to an average in intelligence or physical development.

THE MEDICAL-ILLNESS MODEL OF DEVIANCE

As noted earlier, in practice there are no "pure" models. The configuration of a model and its interrelated elements will be further attenuated when the model is borrowed to fit an entirely different set of problems than those for which it was originally established. Wood notes that the application of the medical-illness model to problems of deviance is an example of "reasoning by analogy in which the model is too often taken for empirical truth without considering how well it applies."[8] One analogy that is highly questionable is the tendency on the part of the human service professional to attribute pathological processes as the cause of deviant behavior. The presence of pathology is frequently merely an inference made by the human service professional upon examining the client's behavior, his or her biography, or the social circumstances involved in the situation. As one observer has written: "Events do not carry with them their own interpretation. They are innocent of any meaning except insofar as we impose it on them."[9]

Therefore "acts of suicide, prostitution, drug usage, and sexual deviance would be categorized as evidence of mental illness. The justification for this distinction is based on the psychoanalytic framework that relates behavior to distortions in the development of the individual's personality from childhood."[10]

The presence of pathology in deviants cannot be detected by examining blood tests and other specimens in the search for disease-causing agents so approximations are developed in their place. These approximations are based on the professional's assessment of how most people behave in various situations and how most people were raised. This line of reasoning represents a switch from an emphasis on detecting pathological processes to an approach that involves utilizing the residual category of normality to detect and understand deviance. When using this assumption one does not ask what a person has in the way of a disease but instead focuses attention on how much or how little the person expresses or experiences a quality that exists in every individual.

As a residual category normality has little actual utility since it is normed on a statistical average and fails to account for compensating factors. A type of statistical index of normality is introduced to replace the known pathological and deteriorating physiological processes found in the medical-illness model. Judgements are then introduced by the human service professional based on a presumed statistical average, that is, how most people behave or how most cases like this one progressed in the past. Questions of adaptation, assimilation, and integration into the fabric of social life are largely ignored, and excessive attention is given to observed or detected differences by the professional. In this way an assumption is made that blindness in an individual makes subsequent dependency a likelihood. Similarly, it is thought, parents of a retarded child are likely to have emotional and adjustment difficulties. One problem with using a statistical approach to detect and treat malfunctioning in individuals is that it does not fit each case, yet inferences are generated about each case as a form of stereotyping by the professional. Parents of retarded children can be just as well adjusted as parents of normal children. Indeed, they will have special problems to overcome but there is no reason to assume that this cannot be accomplished without therapy.

By its very nature a statistical approach arrives at what is "normal" through a calculation of all scores, including the extremes, to determine an average score. For example, at one time it was thought that the average American family consisted of a mother, father, and two children. Yet, most families in the United States are not like this: many families have one adult in the home, or three or more; one child or none, three or more children. A variety of other permutational possibilities exist that represent, when taken together, a majority of the families in the United States.

Other criticisms of the application of the medical-illness model to deviant behavior include the ones mentioned below:

1. "The condition diagnosed as pathogenic is no longer bio-physical, but behavioral; for example, conduct that is judged 'pathological'; and the underlying conditions are also no longer physical, but psychological inferences.... "[11] One can question the validity of applying medical theory and a medical model to problems of conduct. As Andrew Slaby and Lawrence Tancredi observe, there are many deviants who in no way have broken from reality. "They are keenly aware of the prevailing professed mores, and they often assimilate quite well in the society, except for their one, often undetected departure."[12]

2. Unlike most medical judgements, diagnosis and treatment of psychological conditions leads to negative responses by others. Reputations are at stake. To continue to suspect illness in an individual can leave a residue of damaged reputation even when no illness is uncovered.

3. In attempting to get at underlying causes of the behavior rather than treating the symptoms, excessive therapy and, at times, "heroic" treatments are engaged in that are disproportionate to the problem at hand. Unlike the profession of law, neither medicine nor those engaged in the human services have resolved the issue of proportionality. "Let the punishment fit the crime" may seem to be a harsh measure but the other side of this admonition is a warning to exact no more penalties than the crime warrants.

4. Since treatment proceeds from diagnosis, overprediction of

illness (deviance) will lead to iatrogenic illness. Iatrogenic illness can be caused by misdiagnosis and the application of incorrect therapeutic practice as well as the side effects of drugs.*

5. There are few, if any, known and proven standards of treatment for many types of deviance. Mental illness is treated by somatacists and psychotherapists in entirely different ways. Alcoholism is treated medically by physicians and as a problem of "will" by the inspirational-repressive Alcoholics Anonymous. Delinquency, prostitution, and drug addiction have been treated through psychoanalytic technique, group therapy, milieu therapy, hypnotism, and confrontation therapy at various times and places. While there is some agreement that nondirective therapies do not work well with these groups, there is little agreement about anything else.

6. A rarity in medical practice, even with its array of proven techniques is the application of treatment to involuntary patients. Typically, the medical patient can select his or her physician, reject the diagnosis, and terminate the relationship. Interestingly, this is also true of the individual who seeks psychotherapy from a professional in private practice. It is very rare, however, that all of these same rights are accorded the client in human service organizations, and in some agencies and programs none of these rights are available.

7. In human service work clinical judgements typically occur through an interpersonal process. Factors other than client behavior or condition may materially affect the labeling designation. For example, it has been shown that the socioeconomic status, gender, and race of the client have a direct bearing upon the severity ascribed to his or her "pathology."[13]

8. Labels tend to endure but the positive effects of treatment may not. We have seen how labels affixed to persons tend to become master statuses. Labels such as mental illness, criminal, and alcoholic may persist in the minds of others.

---

*See Richard B. Stuart, *Trick or Treatment: How and When Psychotherapy Fails* (Champaign, IL: Research Press. 1970), for an analysis of iatrogenic illness and psychotherapy.

Official records of these labels tend to exist indefinitely. There have been occasions when individuals seeking political office are dropped from the ticket when the public gains knowledge of their past treatment by psychiatrists. On the other hand, the effectiveness of therapy is hotly contested by scholars and researchers. The results of evaluation studies are inconclusive.*

9. Within the human service professions, treatment processes tend to focus almost exclusively on bringing about behavioral control or personal change in the deviant individual. No systematic effort has been made to specify the social mechanisms which might operate to return the stigmatized individual to a normal and acceptable role in the community.

THE SEARCH FOR AN ALTERNATE MODEL

The medical-illness model fails to fit the parameters of the human service professional's endeavors, intentions, and jurisdiction. As we have seen, it is a model that emphasizes pathology and fails to account for normalcy. The application of the medical-illness model to practice in the human services is based on a theory that makes use of one set of categories for undesirable conduct and fails to establish categories to account for desirable conduct.

Second, the directionality of the model does not match the requirements of practice in the human services in terms of social expectations. Its directionality is pointed toward symptom determination — etiology — treatment of original causes, whereas in the case of deviance management, the direction should be toward adjustment of the individual and amelioration of his or her social circumstances.

Third, the medical-illness model places the source of an individual's social distress within him or her and, by some creative lines of reasoning, both relieves the person from responsibility

---

*See, for example, Henry J. Meyer, Edgar F. Borgatta, and Wyatt C. Jones, *Girls at Vocational High: An Experiment in Social Work Intervention* (New York: Russell Sage Foundation, 1965); and Lamar T. Empey and Steven G. Lubeck, *The Silverlake Experiment: Testing Delinquency Theory and Community Intervention* (Chicago: Aldine Publishing Company, 1971).

while simultaneously placing the blame squarely on the individual. Unlike medical practice, however, when the deviant client fails to "recover," it is not seen as the fault of misdiagnosis or poorly administered treatment or unforseen complications. Blame is placed firmly on the client's failure to cooperate. This is the ultimate moral judgement.

In pursuing the search for an alternate model one should keep in mind the earlier discussion concerning ascribed status. Label designations by human service professionals tend to transform individuals into possessing confirmed, negative, master statuses. Since many clients of the human services begin treatment with existing marginal statuses, such as being poor, this confirmed master status can cause considerable additional strain. In addition, because audiences exaggerate and generalize from the single attribute being observed as deviance to include many traits that may not be grounded in fact, the individual is viewed by others as being far more different than he or she really is. This interaction of label, audience, and self works against any possibility of reintegration. An alternative model, therefore, should be capable of minimizing the likelihood of negative status designations.

An additional attribute of the alternative model is that it should be *ahistorical.* Wood notes that:

> Ahistorical therapists claim that a great deal of time is wasted in complet-
> ing ... life histories; that accurate knowledge of the patient's experiences
> several decades ago cannot be obtained; that the past cannot be changed;
> and that most of all, the case history data are not required for treatment.
> Ahistorical counseling is based, for instance, on the discovery of what is
> emotionally disturbing today ... and treating this condition in terms of
> the present situation to which adjustment is sought.[14]

In addition, it should be recalled that typical biographical search procedures employed by professionals are harmful in that they lead to "retrospective interpretation," which tends to convince the individual that he or she was deviant all along.

In summary, then, the alternative model should have the following characteristics:

1. It should be useful in explaining both deviant and nondeviant behavior.
2. The directionality should be toward adjustment, and the

procedures utilized should represent steps or approximations directly related to what the state of adjustment is likely
to be. The model should lead to the professional focusing on
the present reality and future adjustment of the individual.
3. The model should present labels that are free of status
   designations. Where labels are needed they should be descriptions of behaviors rather than persons.
4. The model should be as free as possible of questions of moral
   culpability for the behavior to be changed and for the success
   or failure of the procedures to be employed.

THE BEHAVIORAL APPROACH

In Chapter 2, we discussed psychological theories of deviant
behavior and included among them the behavioral perspective
that is derived from social learning theory. Unfortunately, this
approach suffers from a poor public image since it's often associated
with electroshock, brainwashing, and psychosurgery — procedures
used at an earlier time in the coercive control of deviants. Our
reference to the behavioral approach is entirely concerned with
the body of knowledge and practice known as operant conditioning
and the application of reinforcement procedures to control or
eliminate problems of deviant behavior. In order to avoid recapitu-
lating the principles and procedures of the behavioral approach,
which can be found elsewhere, our discussion is limited to an
examination of the usefulness of this perspective as a model for
understanding and working with deviants.* In other words, how
well does the behavioral approach fit the search for an alternative
to the medical-illness model? The following is a look at the
behavioral approach in terms of desirable characteristics:

1. Usefulness in Explaining Deviant and Nondeviant Behavior

"The view presented (in this approach) . . . is that human behavior is not dichotomous but rather can and should be dealt with
through a single set of principles."[15] As noted in Chapter 2, a basic

---

*See, for example, Ronald L. Akers, *Deviant Behavior: A Social Learning Approach*, 2nd ed.
(Belmont, California: Wadsworth Publishing Co., 1977).

principle of the behavioral perspective is that the distinction between "normal" and "abnormal" behavior is no more than an inference drawn by the observer, no such differences inhere in the behavior itself. The same principles that govern the learning of "normal" behavior also apply to the learning of "abnormal" behavior. The societal reaction to "abnormal" behavior may set in motion social processes that result in a label designation such as juvenile delinquent, shoplifter, or alcoholic. This sanctions intervention by the human service professional by legitimizing the steps to be taken to alter the behavior.

In providing an assessment of the deviant behavior, human service professionals are advised to "describe acceptable behaviors as fully as they describe unacceptable behaviors. Constructive behaviors are likely to be more numerous and more socially important than unacceptable behaviors."[16] Such processes as "retrospective interpretation" and deviant "role engulfment" may still occur since the professional using a behavioral approach does not and cannot control the client's world but by focusing equally on acceptable behaviors the professional does not contribute to the occurrence of these processes.

2. Directionality of Treatment

A distinction is made in this perspective between the conditions that led to the original development of the undesirable behavior and the conditions that currently maintain undesirable behavior. Whenever possible, the intervention is directed at altering the maintaining conditions rather than obviating the original cause. So-called symptoms are treated in this approach with the purpose of changing overt behavior, and such changes frequently produce generalized behavioral effects. The direction of treatment is toward present and future adjustment, rather than providing the client with a "better" understanding of his or her past. A "requirement of clinically useful frameworks is that they must be parsimonious. They must include only such information as is necessary for effective decision-making. In a great many instances it is possible to successfully treat patients for problems whose etiologies are unknown."[17]

The assessment or diagnostic phase is not separated from the treatment phase as is found in historical therapies with their emphasis on the client's biography. "In a diagnostic procedure for behavior modification, the therapist asks a limited number of general questions." One set of questions will focus on measures of the frequency of the target behavior, those to be changed or those to be developed, that will be used as part of the therapy to decide whether the procedures are being successful.[18]

3. The Labels Used Should be Free of Status Designations

When the individual is given a diagnosis under the medical model, he or she receives a negative label owing to the pathological character of the clinical nosology.[19] While this effect can be mitigated somewhat by the individual assuming a "sick role," the perceived punishments involved in relinquishing this role can promote "sick role" continuation. On the other hand, the guiding principle of operant behavioral therapy is that behavior can be modified by altering its environmental consequences. The focus is placed on providing reinforcement contingent on the occurrence of appropriate behavior.[20] For the most part, there is no requirement for any labeling whatever since procedures in this approach are invariably couched in descriptive language. The emphasis is on "what" rather than "why," thereby reducing the potential for moral interpretations by the professional. "In assessment 'what' questions are more likely to lead to behavioral answers than 'why' questions."[21] For example, early in behavior therapy the professional will ask, "What is it about yourself that you would like to change?" Further questions would follow to gain greater specification needed for treatment planning, such as:

"What behaviors would you like to increase in frequency?"
"What behaviors would you like to decrease?"

4. Free of Questions of Moral Culpability

The language used in this approach has objectifiable meaning. Phrases that connote moral failing such as "impulsive," "immature," and "passive" are not used since "they simply contain information about how an observer evaluates the actions and are not descriptions of behavior."[22] Since the premise in this approach is that behavior is a function of the contingencies in the environment, then labeling symptoms, behaviors, or patterns as manifestations of some underlying process is not even considered. The question asked by the behavioral therapist is "What are the controlling contingencies, reinforcements, and punishments operating within the individual's environment?" When the answers to these questions have been discovered, the therapist has completed a functional analysis of the individual's relevant behaviors.[23]

It is at this point that a "moral" decision must be made. Who and what is to be changed? Since the environment is said to control the individual's behavior, is it the school system, the family, or the ascribed deviant, in the case of a child, who is to receive the central attention of the therapist? Like all therapies the behavioral approach is fundamentally conservative and therefore the deviant, not the sustaining social conditions, is most likely to become the target of change.

In summarizing it can be concluded that the behaviorists have a healthy distrust for diagnostic labels. They find them vague and inexplicit as well as used inconsistently by other human service professionals. In regard to deviant behavior they see labeling as resulting in the submergence of positive aspects of the individual's existence along with undue attention to the negative aspects. Furthermore, labels are seen as being so broad as to have no particular value in guiding the choice or course of treatment. Also, mislabeling is seen as a frequent occurrence that can have iatrogenic consequences.

REFERENCES

1. L. Arnold, "Is This Label Necessary?" *The Journal of School Health*, 43: 510–514, 1973.
2. Peter Conrad and Joseph W. Schneider, *Deviance and Medicalization* (St. Louis, Missouri: The C.V. Mosby Company, 1980) p. 17.
3. Conrad and Schneider, *Deviance and Medicalization*, pp. 246–48.
4. Arthur Lewis Wood, *Deviant Behavior and Control Strategies* (Lexington, Massachusetts: Lexington Books, D. C. Heath and Company, 1974) p. 147.
5. Robert A. Scott, "The Construction of Conceptions of Stigma by Professional Experts," in *Deviance and Respectability*, ed. Jack D. Douglas (New York: Basic Books, 1970) p. 286.

6. George Engel, "The Need for a New Medical Model: A Challenge for Biomedicine," *Science, 196* (4296) (April 8): 129–36, 1977.
7. Wood, *Deviant Behavior,* pp. 147–48.
8. Wood, *Deviant Behavior,* p. 148.
9. Leon H. Levy, *Psychological Interpretation* (New York: Holt, Rinehart and Winston, Inc., 1963) p. 8.
10. Andrew Slaby and Lawrence Tancredi, *Collusion for Conformity* (New York: Jason Aronson, 1975) p. 22.
11. Wood, *Deviant Behavior,* p. 148.
12. Slaby and Tancredi, *Collusion for Conformity,* p. 23.
13. Richard B. Stuart, *Trick or Treatment: How and When Psychotherapy Fails* (Champaign, IL: Research Press, 1970) p. 73.
14. Wood, *Deviant Behavior,* p. 149.
15. Leonard Ullman and Leonard Krasner, *A Psychological Approach to Abnormal Behavior* (2nd ed.) (Englewood Cliffs, New Jersey: Prentice-Hall, 1975) p. 5.
16. Stuart, *Trick or Treatment,* p. 182.
17. Stuart, *Trick or Treatment,* p. 182.
18. Ullman and Krasner, *A Psychological Approach* (2nd ed.), p. 220.
19. Stuart, *Trick or Treatment,* p. 103.
20. Steven Reiss and others, *Abnormality: Experimental and Clinical Approaches* (New York: Macmillan Publishing Co., Inc., 1977) p. 207.
21. Ullman and Krasner, *A Psychological Approach* (2nd. ed.), p. 221.
22. Stuart, *Trick or Treatment,* p. 184.
23. Stuart, *Trick or Treatment,* p. 192.

Chapter 8

BEYOND PSYCHOLOGICAL MODELS
The Responsible Professional

PROCEDURAL SAFEGUARDS

Both the medical–illness model and the behavioral approach are "case models" in which case methods are used to focus on problems that are individualized; that is, both the definition of the problem and its intended resolution relate to the need for personal change. Decisions made by professionals that require other people to change their ways are essentially of a moral nature. Jack Kahn and Elspeth Earle put the matter into an appropriate perspective when they note that

> The use of the term "disorder" . . . is the enemy of clear thinking. There is a hidden implication that the disorder is a disease entity which has its form of expression, its recognizable signs, its internal characteristics, and its recognized treatment and possible preventative measures. . . . It must be emphasized that deviation is a departure from standards which are a product of the culture and the criteria are inevitably subjective. There could be no call for intervention unless the values of goodness and badness are applied. A behaviour disorder is behavior which is disapproved. In some cases the behaviour can be judged by religious criteria and referred to as "sinful". If legal standards are applied to the same behaviour it is termed "delinquency". If it becomes termed "behaviour disorder" in a diagnostic framework the implication is that the behaviour is illness. The choice of the context determines the consequence. Sinfulness requires expiation, reparation, or absolution. Delinquency implies the processes of law with its punitive, retributive, and deterrant intentions. Illness implies treatment and a freedom from personal responsibility for the behavior.[1]

Human service professionals tend to assume the role of social control agents by subtly persuading the client that his or her distress is internally generated. In reality, problems of deviance

164

are invariably interactional, that is, they originate with audiences that observe or respond to the behavior in question and are exacerbated through organized social reaction to the deviant. Therefore, solutions arrived at through case-method approaches are unlikely to be entirely successful in the long run. It is those very groups and audiences who intensify and prolong the problems that the deviant faces that the human service professional possesses the least power to influence. Being faced with the dilemmas of having inadequate concepts, tools, and strategies to resolve problems of deviance the professional nevertheless finds no dearth of cases. The daily work goes on.

Ultimately, each person is responsible for his or her own behavior and, with this in mind, a guiding principle for professional conduct can be found in the ancient medical proverb *primum non nocere*, first of all do no harm. Since "harm" as well as "good" is among the possibilities of treatment outcomes, the professional should identify and develop means of maximizing clients' choices in treatment situations. The first remedy for minimizing the potential for harm is information, sufficient to allow the client to make reasonably intelligent choices. Freidson identifies an important consequence of hospital treatment of patients when he notes that

> The patient's understanding is also formed by the sense he himself can make of what is happening to him in the treatment setting. Since the treatment setting is presumably dominated by specialized, expert procedures, however, the most critical source of his information and understanding lies in the staff and its ability and inclination to communicate with the patient. If the staff does not communicate to the patient the meaning of and justification for what is done to him, it in essence refuses him the status of a responsible adult, or of a person in the full sense of the word.[2]

The first procedural safeguard, therefore, is providing information to clients. The human service professional has a duty to communicate to the client an honest representation of his or her skills and the methods that are to be utilized, along with the conditions that are expected to occur during treatment. Expectations for the client's participation should be identified, and, in effect, the anticipated combination of professional/client interactions should form the basis for a written or verbal contract between both parties.

Second, the professional should recognize that it is possible to look at undesirable conduct engaged in by the client without recourse to the mystification of medical–illness diagnosis. Unless required by law, the client should have the right to refuse the label designation. All too often, the professional arrives at a label designation, checks it off on an insurance form or registry and fails to inform the client. If informing the client of the label means that he or she might terminate treatment, so be it. This kind of honesty requires a conviction on the professional's part that the arena of label designating is a moral enterprise. "In a democracy, such an enterprise belongs to the people and those to whom magisterial functions have been delegated by the people. To assign this task to physicians and their surrogates is to give power to a select group who have demonstrated no special competence as moralists."[3] In place of medical–illness diagnoses, behavioral labels should be used. One key advantage in the use of behavior descriptors is that they do not endure forever. Unlike the terms *alcoholic* or *oral personality*, which label a person and imply that he or she can never change, such terms as *frequently engages in fighting behavior* or *heavy drinking behavior* imply that the person is irreducible, and only his or her acts can be classified.

Third, there is a recognized need for procedural safeguards for all clients who enter into treatment with human service professionals. There is no general body of law concerning the human service professions. At the same time the need for safeguards that would protect the individual against the excessive restraint of the police has long been recognized in American courts of law. There are rules to control every aspect of a police officer's interaction with an alleged legal deviant. They pertain to the reasons why the subject is detained for longer than a few minutes, the type of questions the officer may address to the suspect, and the requirements for a clear charge if the officer decides to proceed further.

No equivalent set of rules govern the human service professional who, like the police officer, professes an abiding interest in community welfare and safety. A parallel can be drawn between the lack of clients' rights today and the situation facing the Supreme Court ten to fifteen years ago regarding the inadequacy of procedural safeguards in the juvenile court process. By paraphrasing Justice Fortas' words in the *Kent* case we can arrive at a telling description of the situation, "There is evidence, in fact, that there may be grounds for concern that the [client] receives the worst of both worlds: that he gets neither the protection accorded to [criminals] nor the solicitous care and regenerative treatment postulated for [the physically ill]."[4]

On the organizational level, administrative procedures in public and private human service organizations should be created for case review, appeal, and reducing grievances of clients. The establishment of case review procedures is particularly vital due to the frequency of, and potential for, diagnostic error. In addition, since the diagnosis generally reflects the initial impressions of the client by the professional, it should be modified and improved upon as more and better information is forthcoming. Since there is a tendency for the professionals to "stick with" these initial impressions due to the processes involved in stereotyping, case review by peers or superiors in the organization can serve to reduce the possibility of the same erroneous diagnosis following the client throughout his or her career in the service organization.

The right of appeal of administrative decisions within a bureaucracy is a fundamental aspect of human rights in a democracy. Professionals have been able to protect themselves from having to justify their decisions by claiming the possession of specialized knowledge and the need for autonomy. As Friedson observes, however, even in the most professionalized area of work in our society, that of the health field, "many of the rigid, mechanical, and authoritarian attributes . . . said to characterize the health services may stem more from its professional organization than from its bureaucratic characteristics."[5] The establishment of machinery for handling appeals should provide allowances and guidelines for making the distinction between matters concerning administrative policy and convenience and those concerning actual professional case judgements.

Yet another rationale for the provision of appeal procedures is the tendency of human service professionals to discount clients' complaints and interpret them as a factor of resistance to treatment or as yet another indication of the symptomology for which the client is being treated. On these occasions clients are deemed to have motives but not minds, and there is no recourse within the dyadic treatment situation by which the client can require the professional to reconsider his or her judgement. The existence of appeal machinery within the organization permits a refocusing of the grievance or complaint so that the rights of the client and not his or her character, can take center stage. Furthermore, its availability may also serve to sensitize the recalcitrant professional to the rights of clients simply to avoid being embarrassed.

UNCERTAINTY

The human service professional often finds himself or herself working in an arena filled with uncertainty. Uncertainty as to determining the correct diagnosis of a client, deciding the proper course of treatment, anticipating the length and extent of treatment, and the likelihood of positive case progress and beneficial outcomes. Indeed, this may be one reason why the medical-illness model has become so appealing to the human service professional since it is known to have led to significant advances in medical practice and has achieved some success through its practitioners in improving the general health of the community. So, to a considerable extent, it is grasped at largely through the use of metaphoric language by the human service professional.

The fact that there are no specific cures for most of the illnesses that afflict people in the United States, such as virus diseases, heart disease, and mental illness, does not diminish the value of the model in the eyes of the human service professional. To the contrary, these unknowns in medical practice are said to parallel and exemplify the very problems that human service professionals face. There is no cure for cancer, although it can be arrested, and its etiology is unknown. An analogy can then be drawn between cancer, virus disease, and the diverse behavioral and cognitive "disorders" that human service professionals deal with.

As we have noted, however, the analogy is one that is faulty and reductionistic on two counts. Organic disorders and so-called psychological disturbances cannot be equated since we know very little about the latter. The natural courses of psychological disturbances are largely unknown, generally erratic, and subject to a considerable degree of modification based upon contextual factors such as environmental and interpersonal situations and conditions. Furthermore, a large proportion of such disturbances may not be psychogenic at all but instead are caused or shaped by social conditions. Knowledge of the origins of behavioral deviations is even less developed.

Second, the anticipation of achieving an eventual "breakthrough" in the treatment of such disturbances is largely a myth. The breakthrough imagery is what has popularized medical science. The achievement of miraculous cures for death dealing diseases has played a very small role in achieving longevity of the population or improving the general health of the community. The major drop in the death rates from infectious diseases, for example, took place long before the introduction of antibiotics and other specific remedies and preventatives. The increased life span of the population in the United States in the past century has been due primarily to better food and water and improved hygiene and sewage disposal. Even were breakthroughs to occur they would most likely only be applicable to a very small proportion of the deviant population and would most likely arise from developments in other fields, such as genetics and biochemistry.

Uncertainty will continue to rule decisions by the human service professional for now and in the foreseeable future. This situation should be faced squarely, and guidelines need to be developed. Witkin suggests that many of the skills required of an effective researcher are equally necessary to the professional and will lead to a reduction in the error rate.[6] While this approach is commendable, it says little about the need for a set of over-arching self-imposed rules or guidelines that the professional can utilize in making decisions. An exploration of some facets of uncertainty situations should help to clarify the issue.

Uncertainty is a state that can be defined as not sure or certain in knowledge; doubtful, not definite; or vague. Error is most likely to occur when uncertainty is present and the professional must nevertheless take some action, such as making a labeling decision. The following are action possibilities that inhere in uncertainty situations:

a. to underact
b. to overact
c. to do nothing

To take exactly the correct action would be fortuitous in such situations, since, by definition, uncertainty means that the right action is unknown to the actor.

Uncertainty and resulting error has frequently been attributed to a deficit in information. If only we had more and perhaps better information about a client's past life, we might be better able to help her handle the present. This type of thinking captures but half the problem. It is the future that remains unknown, regardless of one's knowledge of past events. Uncertainty implicitly refers to an unknown future in this formulation.

Therefore, a characteristic of situations in which uncertainty is present is the need for the professional to base his or her actions on a prediction of the client's behavior in the future. Human service professionals, as we have seen, tend to overpredict deviant behavior, that is, they seem to favor the second action possibility, overacting.

A case model that offers an opposite approach has been proposed by Thomas J. Scheff. The decision rule in law for arriving at decisions in the face of uncertainty is that "a man is innocent until proven guilty." Sheff indicates that under English common law this means "that the judge or jury must find the evidence of guilt compelling beyond a reasonable doubt." When doubt does exist the decision should be to acquit the defendant.[7]

As Scheff notes:

The jury or judge must not be equally wary of erroneously convicting or acquitting: the error that is most important to avoid is to erroneously convict.... The reasons underlying this rule seem clear. It is assumed that in most cases, a conviction will do irreversible harm to an individual by damaging his reputation in the eyes of his fellows. The individual is seen as weak and defenseless, relative to society, and therefore in no position to sustain the consequences of an erroneous decision. An erroneous acquittal, on the other hand, damages society.... Although [there may be] serious outcomes they are generally thought not to be as serious as the consequences of erroneous conviction for the innocent individual, since society is able to sustain an indefinite number of such errors without serious consequences. For these and perhaps other reasons, the decision rule to assure innocence exerts a powerful influence on legal proceedings.[8]

PROFESSIONAL RESPONSIBILITY

While the process of arriving at labeling decisions may be frequently characterized by an aura of uncertainty the labels as they are affixed to individuals are a final product. The dispensing of labels is a relatively straightforward and unregulated activity almost totally controlled by the professional. In those rare circumstances where labeling is contested, such as criminal trials where the defendant claims insanity as a defense, specialists such as psychiatrists and psychologists are brought into the picture to testify on both sides of the issue. Labeling in this context represents the "opinions" of specialists while the "facts" are determined by a judge or a jury composed of the defendant's peers. Decisions, in this context, are then made by an individual or group of neutral persons following guidelines established under the law. The judge or the jury selects from among the theories presented by opposing attorneys and the opinions presented by opposing experts those that seem to best represent the truth.

In most other contexts, however, the labeling process is entirely unregulated and uncontested. In situations where the labeled individual desires to contest the decision there is rarely a procedure for doing so. If human service professionals wish to retain their uncontested ability to perform labeling, some guidelines for self-regulation will have to be developed. Unless this is accomplished it is likely that we will see an increase in litigation, largely of a civil law nature, and, perhaps ultimately, regulation by the courts.

There is at least one useful model from which guidelines can be evolved and applied to labeling decisions performed by human service professionals. The various standards of proof found in law and utilized by the courts are, in effect, guidelines that take into account the risk of error in legal judgments. Standards of proof represent the degree to which a party in a lawsuit must support its allegations. In addition, they reflect not only the weight of private and public interests but a societal judgment about how the risk of error should be distributed between litigants.

It is not this author's proposal that the trappings of the court be brought into the human service organization or that the act of labeling an individual closely resemble a verdict of guilty in a criminal trial. However, since reputations and intrusion into people's lives are at stake, the possibility of harm accompanying an erroneous label is ever present. Mislabeling or false labeling must therefore be guarded against.

In a criminal proceeding where an individual's liberty is at risk, the state must establish its case "beyond a reasonable doubt." Our constitutional heritage requires that when there is a threat to liberty there must be due process of law before any deprivation occurs. The standard of proof, "beyond a reasonable doubt," should then be the guideline adhered to by the human service professional in recommending involuntary commitment of those persons thought to be mentally ill, mentally retarded and other developmentally disabled persons, narcotics addicts, and alcoholics. Suspicion that such illnesses and addictions are present is insufficient; there must be overwhelming evidence that these conditions have been of long-standing duration and are clearly injurious to self and others.

Within the law pertaining to civil suits, the interests of the defendant are of a lesser magnitude, therefore, a case can be determined by a mere "preponderance of evidence." This guideline allows for a greater risk of error than "reasonable doubt" and should therefore be applied in those labeling situations where loss of liberty is not at issue. Actually, this standard or guideline within the law is the least stringent, allowing for the greatest chance of error, and is typically used in cases involving monetary loss or gain. Therefore, other issues pertaining to due process, such as depriving or interrupting freedom of association of a child in a public school through placement in a special class or program should require a higher standard of proof. Similarly, where labeling may lead to any form of coercive treatment this standard should not be used. The "preponderance of evidence" standard applies best to those situations where the client is able to provide informed consent, where the results of error will likely lead to minor consequences, and where treatment can be terminated unilaterally by the client.

Between "beyond a reasonable doubt" and "preponderance of evidence" guidelines lies a third, which is an intermediate standard of proof. Known as "clear and convincing evidence" it is a guideline that suggests the need for reasonable, but not absolute, certainty in arriving at labeling decisions that are based upon strong, supporting documentation. This standard is particularly applicable to those situations involving harm to another party such as in the determination of child abuse or neglect. The suspicions, insights, and guesses of the human service professional are insufficient support for this standard. It requires the results of tests, eyewitness reports of the behavior in question, personal testimony that is supported by physical evidence, or physical evidence alone that can be linked to the behavior in question.

To summarize, the risk of error in labeling should be related to a standard of proof:

Standard of proof	*Risk of error*
Preponderance of evidence	High
Clear and convincing evidence	Medium
Beyond a reasonable doubt	Low

Models available to the human service professions, particularly the medical–illness model, fail to take into account the harm that may befall clients through labeling. Applying the entire constitutional Bill of Rights to the human service professional's domain would be overly restrictive and make treatment of clients next to impossible. Therefore, since clients' rights rest in the hands of the professional, the professional also assumes the responsibility for protecting these rights. Appropriate guidelines can be drawn from procedural safeguards that now exist in the criminal law. For example, in an increasing number of states, professionals must report suspected cases of child abuse to an official investigatory or sanctioning agency. In an average voluntary, family counseling agency, information about abuse may be revealed coincident with a focus on other problems. Since the professional, by law, must report this information, should he or she have alerted the husband

and wife to this requirement at the time of the first interview? This would simply be the application of the Miranda warning that the police use prior to questioning a suspect.

Such questions are merely intended to be provocative. There are no easy answers to the question of how a balance can be achieved between protecting clients' rights and the harm that may befall those clients and society should energetic pursuit of these rights prevent treatment.

CONCLUSION

The rights of people in a free society are significantly reduced when powerful groups are able to ascribe statuses irrespective of the needs or wishes of the individuals involved. As we have seen, deviance designations are more likely to be ascribed than achieved. Each designation leaves its distinctive mark on the person it touches. Many labels cast the person so designated as being subhuman. Others are milder but mark the label bearers as being irresponsible or immature or as being incapable of making intelligent decisions in their own behalf.

The ease of designating someone as deviant is not matched by a corresponding mode of removing that label from the person. We do not have special ceremonial rites of passage that clearly mark the termination of deviant status, the resumption of a nondeviant identity, and the readmission of the individual to an honorable position in the social order. The creation of deviants is a relatively simple matter. Turning these persons into nondeviants is far more difficult, and at times impossible, since it involves forces beyond the control of the human service professional.

Harold Bursztajn and others, have written a provocative book that deals with uncertainty in medical diagnosis and practice.[9] They present a case early in the book that exemplifies the frustrations faced by physicians when they cannot label a patient's condition. It is the case of a hospital patient, a boy just under two years of age, who shows signs of improving shortly before his death. A factor contributing to the child's death is the invasive diagnostic measures utilized by the physicians in efforts to discover the cause of illness. The authors pose a number of questions they believe should be asked of physicians prior to embarking on a course of intrusive diagnostic procedures: "How likely is this to do good? How likely is it to do harm?... What in this situation is good? Whose good are we working for? What is best for the patient? What does the patient want?"[10]

Similar questions should be asked by each human service professional as he or she begins to work with a client. The "divine rights" of royalty in the middle ages should not be replicated in the powers granted to professionals in the twentieth century to bestow lesser statuses on troublesome and suffering persons.

REFERENCES

1. Jack Kahn and Elspeth Earle, *The Cry For Help* (Elmsford, New York: Pergamon Press, 1982).
2. Eliot Freidson, "Dominant Professions," in *Human Service Organizations*, eds. Yeheskel Hasenfeld and Richard A. English (Ann Arbor: University of Michigan Press, 1974) p. 435.
3. Theodore R. Sarbin and James C. Mancuso, *Schizophrenia: Medical Diagnosis or Moral Victory* (New York: Pergamon Press, 1980) p. 220.
4. *Kent V. United States*, 383 U.S. 541, 555–56 (1966).
5. Freidson, "Dominant Professions," p. 431.
6. Stanley L. Witkin, "Cognitive Processes in Clinical Practice," *Social Work*, 27(5)(September): 389–395, 1982.
7. Thomas J. Scheff, *Being Mentally Ill* (Chicago: Aldine Publishing Company, 1966) p. 107.
8. Scheff, *Being Mentally Ill*, p. 107.
9. Harold Bursztajn and others, *Medical Choices, Medical Chances: How Patients, Families and Physicians Can Cope With Uncertainty* (New York: Delacorte Press/ Seymour Lawrence, 1981).
10. Bursztajn and others, *Medical Choices, Medical Chances*, p. 17.

INDEX

Diet
juvenile delinquency and, 68
Dietrick, Raymond, 95
Dillon, Marcia, 41
Disabilities, physical (*see* Handicaps, physical)
Disease
definition of, 22
illness versus, 152–153
Divoky, Diane, 91, 97, 133
Divorce
social deviance study compared to, 3–4
Douglas, Jack D., 6, 24
DSM–III, 65
criticisms of, 65, 90–91
purpose of, 65
Dunham, H. Warren, 47, 52
Durkheim, Emile, 48, 52

E

Earle, Elspeth, 164, 175
Eaton, Joseph W., 71, 72, 95
Effective cause
definition of, 76
Empey, Lamar T., 157
Engel, George, 163
English, Richard A., 147
Esco, Jack, 130, 147
Ethnocentrism, 128–130, 132, 134
Etzioni, Amitai, 119, 120, 121, 146

F

False positive (*see also* Mislabeling)
definition of, 131
Faris, Robert E. L., 47, 52
Ferdinand, Theodore N., 36, 40, 41
Ferman, Louis A., 130, 146
Fingerprint patterns
crime and, 68
Formal labels
current use in United States, 60
definition of, 58
informal labels versus, 78–79
labeling theory and, 77–79
organizations and, 83
Fortas, Abe, 167

Fort Lauderdale, 125
Foster, Madison, 130, 146
Freedman, Jonathan L., 86, 96
Freidson, Eliot, 25, 31, 40, 63, 95, 140, 147, 165, 167, 175
Freud, Anna, 29, 40

G

Gagnon, John H., 146
Gambling
classification as disease, 89
Gelles, Richard H., 69, 95, 97
Gibbons, Don C., 51, 52, 53, 96
Gil, David, 69, 95
Gittelman, Rachel, 145, 148
Glaser, Daniel, 5, 10, 24
Goffman, Erving, 82, 96, 115, 117
Goldstein, Joseph, 29, 40
Goode, Erich, 43, 51, 52, 53, 85, 94, 96
Goodwin, Donald W., 25
Gordon, J. E., 41
Gove, Walter R., 107, 117
Guze, Samuel B., 25

H

Handicaps, physical
problems associated with
example of, v–vi
social deviance versus, 9–10
Hasenfeld, Yeheskel, 139, 140, 147
Height
social deviance and, 9
Hindelang, M. J., 95
Hingson, Ralph, 97
Hostetler, John A., 72
Human service organizations
bureaucratization and, 140
coercive power and, 120
distinctions among, 136–138
labeling theory and, 83–84
labels and, 68–70
mistreatment of children and, 22–23
professionalization and, 138–139, 140
promotion of deviance by, 83, 84
self-image of clients and, 83
self-serving activities and, 84
social deviance and, 14